WESTENDERS

Memories of Benwell, Elswick, Scotswood & Arthur's Hill

Yvonne Young

This book is dedicated to the memory of

Bella Hull and Nancy Shields

True Local Lasses

And also to everyone who raised funds for the
Bobby Robson Cancer Fund

Bella Hull who lived in Elswick and was known and loved by everyone.

Nancy Shields (née Nichol, previously Rice) – a great friend.

Previous page: South Benwell School pupils all together in the yard on a sunny day. Betty Atkin (née Brannen) is fifth from the right front row. Also included are: Connie Barclay, Fred Armstrong and D. Kettle.

Front cover, bottom picture: Scotswood folk outside a shop in Chapel Terrace in 1936.

Copyright Yvonne Young 2010

First published in 2010 by

Summerhill Books
PO Box 1210, Newcastle-upon-Tyne NE99 4AH

www.summerhillbooks.co.uk

Email: summerhillbooks@yahoo.co.uk

ISBN: 978-1-906721-29-9

Printed by Martins the Printers Ltd, Berwick upon Tweed

Contents

Introduction

Over the past year, during research for this book I have met the most amazing characters. Many of them are included in this book. But, in the process, I could have written another dozen like it, simply because the people of the West End have lived such fascinating lives. I find myself thinking "I wish that I could include Mr So and So or Mrs Such and Such." Initially after completing my first book *Benwell Remembered*, I had intended to make it part of a set – Benwell, Elswick then Scotswood, but this book will include those areas and touching on Arthur's Hill, Westgate and Fenham.

You all have a story. I would encourage you all to write them down, especially the memories of your parents. I always regret not having asked enough questions when mine were alive. I've held interviews with older residents when their children have been present and I've heard them say things like "I didn't know that you worked there." Or heard them gasp to hear about their parent's role during World War Two. People ask me how I write, as if it's some elusive activity. I say "Write the way you speak, we are all natural storytellers." When we talk about where we've been for our holidays, our first job or an embarrassing moment – it flows naturally.

There are important changes taking place in Benwell, Elswick and Scotswood. St James' Church is becoming a Heritage Centre and there will be much more going on for locals. Search is organising more trips, training and advice sessions. Riverside Community Health Project is supporting valuable activities and events. There are lots of groups who raise funds for causes, Small Sparks, Scotswood Diner, Cornerstone, Benwell Hall, Ferguson's Lane Club and many others.

The West End Library continues to be a major focus in the community offering activities, films, music and book launches. They form links with schools and groups in the area.

I'm proud to be a "Westender".

Yvonne Young
2010

Centre Street – King George V Silver Jubilee Party in 1935.

Wait Till I Get Turned Around
by Olive Clayton (née Bonner)

Olive Bonner was born at 67 Buddle Road in 1949. That group of houses were known as the "Cellar" as they were reached by a flight of stairs below the main road. Her dad Freddie was born in 1912 at Hugh Gardens. "My dad's mam, Granny Bonner lived upstairs to Maureen Clark and Charlie Watson. Dad worked for Armstrong's as a fitter and turner at the Elswick Works. Me and my sister Gladys went down to the factory when they had an open day. The factory was showing off all of the equipment they had made and we had a turn sitting inside a tank. It was murder climbing onto the top, but we really enjoyed the experience."

From left to right: Phil Simons, Peter Moore, Pepi the poodle and Olive Bonner on the corner of Maughan Street and Buddle Road.

Olive remembered some of the people who lived nearby. In the winter her mam would tell Gladys and Olive to shovel snow away from the doors of their neighbours. "Florrie Duck lived near where the butchers shop was and when we had done the work she came to the front door with an orange each for us, but we were never invited in. Scotch Lambert lived upstairs to Florrie. There were the Aisbitt's, Sally and John – they didn't have any kids. She always used condensed milk and John put it on his bread, I had a taste one day and loved it so I started to eat it at home. They introduced me to scallions, they put salt on them. I'd never tasted them before and thought they were lovely. I went straight home to ask mam to buy some. I tried rhubarb dipped in sugar and I was always on at my mam to buy it."

Olive babysat for Betty who lived a few doors along from Jacky White's fish shop. She sometimes saw Jacky sitting in his chair outside in the sun. "He always looked very healthy with a tan. Jean Beattie ran the bakers next to the post office on Buddle Road, there was a drapers on the corner and Bella Booth's on the other corner. We loved to eat sherbet lemons, midget gems, pineapple chunks and spangles. Mix ups from Mrs Wilson's shop were great. Her shop became Gordon Kinghorn's and he turned it into the first supermarket we had ever seen. It was the first self service where you could help yourself and get tick. Ernie the butcher was next door."

Olive's sister Gladys loved the trips which were organised by Edie Jones. "Mary Brown lived in the flat under Geordie Jones and she had two sons called Arty and Kevin. We used to go on Edie's trips to Tynemouth and Cullercoats. We took our own food and called them seaside sandwiches. Mary used to take a huge tea pot and loose tea with a flask of hot water. As soon as we got back our Glad was asking Edie when she was going to organise the next trip and she always answered with the same phrase "Wait until I get turned around!"

Atkinson Road School Football team. From left to right. Back row: Billy Clayton, Robert Evans, ?, Robert Varley, Doug Marsh, Teacher ? Middle row: Colin Laing, Alan Armstrong, Vena Kapur, Max Livingston, Jeff Mouter. Front row: Angus Errington, David Ekong, Alan Cummings.

"My mam was born in the Scotswood Road area and all of our cousins, aunts and uncles lived on either Aline Street or Violet Street. Our Stephen and Rosa got a house on Amelia Street and he liked a night out at the Old Hall Social Club. In our house we had a big table which stood right in the middle of the room. Mam showed me how to iron clothes. She put the plug into the light fitting on the ceiling, I was on all day. She also used to send me to the shop for a loaf of uncut bread. I loved the smell so much that I used to bite off every corner of the loaf, the family never got an uncut loaf without bites out of the corners. There used to be a bakers shop on Adelaide Terrace, I think it was Carricks, it stood where the pie and pea shop used to be. They sold cakes cheaply after 4 o'clock so me and Glad went up there to buy them for mam, but we always acted about on the way home and the cakes were battered by the time we got there."

Olive attended South Benwell School and then continued her education at Atkinson Road School. She remembered that Miss Campbell was the head teacher in the infants. "When I was about six years old I heard a rumour that there was a ghost in the toilets. We had to walk across the yard to the toilet block and one day I'd asked to go. Someone must have seen me go in there and they made sounds to scare me, I can't remember if I actually used the toilet that day. I was a prefect in the top class of South Benwell. I wore a badge and stood on the stairs to supervise the kids going down to the hall for dinner. Miss Gillespie taught in the juniors. In the winter we were allowed to take our slippers, we changed out of our wellies. That building always felt lovely and warm with those old fashioned radiators. I usually went home for dinner as I lived so near to the school."

Olive and her sister Gladys on the right of the photo watching the game. Florence Malone is reaching for the ball. Author Sid Chaplin looks on from the left with Dunston Power Station in the background. Sid's book 'The Watchers and the Watched' was published in 1962 when this photo was taken. The front cover of the book shows the same view. He was probably in the area to promote his book.

Olive remembered some of the teachers at Atkinson Road School. "I remember Mr Ralph Watson who taught art, he later became an actor. We got Mrs Dinsdale for Geography, Mrs Clarke took Science and PE, English with Mr Bradshaw, Mr Thompson for History, there was also Mr Keys. Mr Dewhirst was headmaster and Mr Bell the deputy. I remember one day I was chattering and carrying on during country dancing and Mr Bell shouted down from the balcony "You girl, in the green stripy shorts … come up to my office!" He told me to sit in the basket as a punishment, he forgot all about me and I was sat there for an hour. Me and Jean Beattie had the job of making tea in the staff room. I met Billy Clayton at school who was later to become my husband."

Cookery lessons, which were referred to as Housecraft lessons were a favourite of Olive's. She remembers her Gondola basket. "I was over the moon when I first bought it. We were asked to buy ingredients to make a Christmas cake, but mam didn't have the money, so Miss Anderson asked me to make her a cake and she would provide the resources. She was quite young and a very pretty teacher. I made a really good job, it wasn't a very large cake, but I covered it with blue and white icing sugar with a sledge decoration on the top. There was a competition to see who had made the best cake and mine won – the prize was chocolates and little scented soaps. Dad was over the moon that I had won and he said "Ask her how much it will cost to buy the cake and give the bairn the money." It was five shillings. I had piped it so beautifully that I didn't want anyone to break into it when I brought it home."

Maths wasn't one of Olive's strong points and she laughs as she recalls one numerical incident. "Me and Barbara Welch weren't very good at problems so we copied each other's work. Mrs Bell asked us to go out to the front of the class to have our work marked. She asked us why our workings out were the same. We got the strap. When I got home, I told mam and she said "Well … you must have deserved it!" I remember that Mrs Bell once broke her leg as she was reaching up to a high shelf to get a book."

Olive made good friendships in Benwell. "Once we decided to take a day off school, I went to Barbara Welch's house with Kathleen Trotter, Sylvia Hall and Sandra Holden. Barbara was cooking us liver and onions for our dinner when there was a knock at the front door. It was my mam, somebody had told her where we were. I never did this again. I remember when jumpers came into fashion with the big diamond patterns, Barbara always wore mohair or lamb's wool and trouser suits which were very smart, we swapped and borrowed each other's clothes. There was a shop facing Dookun's

dentists on Adelaide Terrace which sold lovely twin sets. We didn't wear jeans, mainly tank tops and mini skirts. I really wanted a midi skirt, they were quite long but not full length. I borrowed one from my friend Jennifer Dunn, her brother was nicknamed Sconnie, he delivered newspapers for Reggie Moore."

"Me, Sylvia and Jennifer used to go to the Mayfair afternoon dance in town. There was no alcohol, it was just for teenagers, mam gave me the money. But, when she saw me dressed in the skirt, she ripped it off me saying that I wasn't going out dressed "Like that!" I tried to tell her that it wasn't

Olive and Billy on a night out at Elsie Reed's 50th party. The news of the death of Lady Diana was broadcast on this day.

mine, but it was too late. We also went to the Majestic dance. I wore flat shoes usually and I was really pleased when I got a pair of Cuban heels from a fancy shop. They were French navy, mam kept trying to stop me from wearing them because they were new. I said "Yes, they're new, I know they're new and every bugger else knows that they're new, now shut up mother and get in! I remember a pink blouse I had with bell sleeves and elasticated cuffs, it had a big collar. Kids wore skirts with net under and hoola hoop hems with waistcoats to match. I always wore my hair long. We sometimes went up to Mark Toney's café for an orange juice, it was next to the Bendix wash house."

"When me and Billy first started going out together we met at Bella Booth's shop sometimes. Bella let us sit in her shop and we went for messages for her to the pub at the bottom of Hannah Street, The Gun – she liked a drink of Guinness." Another friend of Olive's was Karen Strong. Her dad had a shop on Scotswood Road – a general dealers. The family lived at Greenhow Place.

Olive's first job at the age of fifteen was for the glass works which was situated above the leatherworks at Railway Terrace along near Vickers. Her cousin secured her an interview. "I was cleaning glass for army goggles. The company made government war equipment. I pushed them through to be washed in a machine and then stacked them between this acetone stuff, then they went down to a furnace which made them stronger. Everyone got a turn to go over the road to buy sandwiches for dinner for everyone. My next job was for a picture framers at Gladstone Street at Byker, I was sixteen. I also worked for W. & H.O. Wills on the Coast Road, meanwhile, Billy was working on the Civic Centre building. The building was nearly finished when we got married there and all of his mates were sitting on the scaffolding throwing pennies from the roof. It was March 1968 and I was 18 and Billy was 20. My friend Elsie was my witness and her boyfriend Eddie, who became her husband. Afterwards we all went to the Café Royal. Mam got us our first house, she went down to Lamb and Edge. The rent was one pound a week, it was at 138 Violet Street."

Olive's friend Barbara had a job at a shop which treated baldness. Her job was to apply oil to the scalp and she was taught how to massage the head. Olive also took a job here. "The shop was on Pilgrim Street near the Police Station. There was a little reception area and we wore white overalls. I didn't stay there long, I thought that I had nearly electrocuted one poor man. I secured the stick on pads which were attached to a machine. He began shaking because I had applied too much current. Billy and I were living with Billy's mother at the time in Cromwell Street beside the Dodsies Arms."

Billy worked on many contracts in Scotland, Holland and one job was scaffolding on the Piper Alpha. "A lad was on his holidays and Billy stepped in to take his place. It was the first time that he had been on this rig. The men did two weeks on and two weeks off. Billy was working on the top level and was in the cinema, he remembered seeing John Scott from Newcastle in there. As Billy was at the top, he had a clear view, so when the explosion happened he was able to jump. I didn't know anything about it until the next day when his sister who was living in Derby rang at 7.30 am to ask "What rig is our Billy on, there has been an accident and one of them has blown up?" When she told me I went temporarily blind with shock. He can't remember jumping and he was hurt when they fished him out of the water, but he was holding a workmate up and asked the rescuers to pick him out first as he was in more need. Billy was recognised by the queen for bravery. Me and our Deborah went with him all dolled up to the palace. He was presented with a gold feathers award which was in a case with a letter. They never found John Scott, but Billy was able to tell his wife where he was last seen.

He still meets up with friends Joe Meenan and Davy Lambert. Joe now lives in Stonehaven, Scotland and Davy lives in Middlesbrough, They meet up every year when they go up to Edinburgh for a few drinks and a meal making a whole day of it.

Olive and Billy now live in Gosforth.

The Claytons lived in Cromwell Street in 1968. This photo was taken in the late 1970s during demolition.

Get Oot O' The Road!
by Matty Bryson

There is some controversy as to whether there were forty nine or fifty pubs along Scotswood Road. But, according to Matty Bryson, who was part of the team responsible for the demolition of the pubs in the 1960s. "There were only four technically. There was a pub or a shop on just about every corner along the road. The four pubs who couldn't claim to be anywhere else were the Hydraulic Crane, the Moulders Arms, Delaval Arms and the Shipwrights. The Gun was at the bottom corner of Enfield Road, the Forge Hammer at Edgeware Road, The Skiff on Railway Street and so on."

Matty also remembers a pub which was opposite the entrance to the Paradise Council Yard. It was known locally as the Skew Bridge. "At one time the Boat House used to be a café owned by Dusty and Gerry, two blokes. There used to be an old drift mine nearby where Jobling Purser's was – they manufactured grease and fertiliser– it became Corus. The mine went under the railway line, Clara Street and Scotswood Road. It had been previously protected by a wire mesh gate, but became unsafe and was bricked up after the deaths of two young lads."

When he came out of the army in 1953 he worked at Lemington Brick Works. Matty's next job was for Purser's. "I also went to work filling up the tankers that went around tarring the roads. I was up at 5.30 am in the morning. We worked on the roads as far as Kielder. When I was at the depot, many people reported hearing noises. Tales went around that it was the ghosts of the two lads. It was probably the dripping and tapping from the old drift mine, but it still sent shivers up the back of my neck on cold dark mornings."

The Boat House (also known as the Skew Bridge). The railway bridge can be seen in the background.

Matty speaks of his work throughout the '60s. He was on the demolition squad which was responsible for clearing Scotswood Road of the many pubs along its route.

"I knocked down pubs and old houses. One of the places was where Jimmy Forsyth lived, it was a downstairs flat with an old style range oven which had a little hearth where the proggy mats lay. At some point, there was some fire damage near the range on the floor boards. There was a little hole and I found some money in there, which must have slipped down there, some tanners, pennies and farthings. I always used to say "I owe Jimmy some money." Jimmy later moved along Aline Street way."

He laughs as he recalls his frequent encounters with Jimmy, the well known local photographer. The team were forever chasing him for his own safety. "He lived on Dickman's Pies – they were quick and easy to eat on his way around taking photos. Every time we saw him eating, it was always a Dickman's. I ate them too – I must have put away thousands of them. Everyone knew when a building was coming down, because Jimmy would be there. Part of my job was to climb inside the house to put a huge wire rope onto the second storey window. We always made sure that nobody was in the building before we placed the bucket on the Caterpillar loader. Jimmy always came back and we would shout "Get oot o' there man!" I would wave at the machine driver, giving the signal and down it would come. A huge cloud of dust would go up, and when it cleared – there was Jimmy standing in the middle like a phantom."

The pub jobs were always designated for Sunday's. Matty would hear someone shout "Get oot o' the road!"

"Jimmy only had one good eye, being blind in the other, so that meant he was temporarily blinded by the dust. The problem was that once the building began to crumble, we couldn't tell which direction it was going to fall. We'd get into the lofts and pop the slates off. One day I was working on the Grapes pub. There was always a carved signature in wood on the pubs. There was a couple of bunches of grapes on a plinth, an American fella approached me and asked if he could buy them. I got ten bob a piece. Another pub I was working on had a set of mock marble pillars. The plywood was curled around into cylinders. A bloke came and asked us if he could buy them, he really thought that they were authentic. There used to be a yard off the garage on Condercum Road which bought stuff for a couple of bob."

"There was a Co-op building at the bottom of Gloucester Street. It became empty and our team was sent to pull it down. We noticed that it had a very fine sun canopy. As we had planned a camping trip, but were in need of a tent, we had the idea to use the canopy. The tents we had used in the past were old army issue and were useless in the rain. Each time they were touched the water came through. We cut it in half to make it easier to handle. Then, sometime later a museum came to the site to enquire where it had disappeared to. They wanted to use it for a display set and we had draped it over our tent.

A view of the old Gloucester Street. The photo was taken in 1960.

Matty remembers the banter that went on during his work. "There were heavy cables under the street lights and when we pulled on the cable, the lamp posts just used to keel over. Next thing, some woman would come running out shouting "You've cut me bloody cooker off." We used to laugh and say "Watch the cooker doesn't come doon the stairs when we pull the main cable." One of the fella's I worked with, Hughie Drinkald, worked on demolition also – seven days a week. After work, he'd go out and get a pile of Chronicles, deliver them at Cowgate, then rush back to the Forresters Arms. On Easter and Bank Holidays he went to market for kippers and those roll mops to sell them along Beaumont Street. He used to shout "Calla Herring." He sold them out of an old pram. One time a woman came out of her house and asked "Are they fresh?"

"Hughie answered "Are they fresh? ... Hinny, they're lying on top of one another!"

"We were working in Lefroy Street near Park Road. A woman came to the top of the back stairs. "You've knocked me Redifusion off!"

"There was a little box on the side of the windowsill and the wire had been pulled out. She demanded that he fixed it. He shouted, "Shut up woman, I'm not an engineer." Then, he knotted the broken wires together. We had some good times. One time when Geordie Bowman wanted to build a garden fence. We took him from Frank Street to Scotswood Road with 12 and 14 feet pieces of wood and 7x2 batons on the roof of a Reliant Robin van. The wood was so heavy that my son Davey had to sit on the bonnet to keep the front wheels of the van on the road. It was ok at first going down the steep bank, but when we hit the bottom, it was a different story. Geordie Bowman's brother Vince is still going strong – he sells cars."

"Geordie Cuthbertson lived on Clumber Street. His was one of the first houses to come down. Then, he moved into the King's Meadows. He used to drink in the Rifle. Jimmy Forsyth knew that we pulled the pubs down on Sundays. We had spent the Saturday gutting the inside of the Rifle and taking the roof off. Overnight, there had been a high wind and the old pub fell down. Jimmy came around the next day and complained that we had pulled it down before he got there. We told him that it had just collapsed, he was gutted."

There were a wide range of working mens clubs in the area. Matty went to the Old Hall, Joan Street Club, Pendower and Fenham clubs which have all now been pulled down. "I went to the Springbank and also the Tavern at Cowgate. I knew some great people. There are still people who won't talk to me to this day because I took part in the demolition of the pubs along Scotswood Road."

Matty was born on Buddle Road above the Co-op Stores at the Edgeware Road end. Two families lived above the stores. "We had the attic rooms and uncle Bob was below us. The front rooms had Dorma style windows with net stretched across on wire. We used to pull the curtain along and use it as a stage. When my mam had enough of the noise, she'd charge upstairs with a cat o' nine tails. She would send me to the shops for a message. I always took my gurd (hoop) I went faster when I took it – I dawdled when I didn't take it."

He remembered that they never used wallpaper. The family used a preparation which was applied in a

Matty's wife, Doreen, with Simba the family dog outside her home on Atkinson Road.

similar way to whitewash, but it was red ochre in colour. "I was about two or three years old. Sunday was the only time we sat at the table together for a meal. Dad was the only one who got custard with his pudding. When he was finished, the bowl was passed around to us kids, our George, Tommy, Margaret and Dolly, by the time it got to me, there was never any left."

Matty speaks of his brother George who later married Florence, they lived above the shop at the bottom of Maughan Street, No 2. The main entrance was from the back lane. (George had daughters Linda and Sandra, Sandra was a good pal of mine in the 1960s.)

"Florence's brother was killed on Scotswood Road. He and a mate were crossing the road to James Street and Northbourne Street. There was a no entrance sign, but a taxi driver mowed into them. Killed one and crippled the other. Our George used to work for Jobling Purser's."

"The Irish workmen used to always say at the end of a shift "It's a day for the sawdust." Meaning time for the pub. We used to play dominoes with them in the Doddsies Arms. We always played 31s, play until we got to 31 – it was one shilling to win. There were five of us, the three Irish blokes were built like brick houses. Us Geordies went outside for a pee and one of the Irish blokes stayed in. When we came back there were two dominoes missing. One of them said to his mate.

"Have you got the dominoes?"

"I have not!"

"You have!"

"I have not … are you calling me a liar?"

"No … but just put them back."

Matty laughed. "He put them back and we got on with the game. They had a great sense of humour. There used to be a canny fella called Mr Barber who lived on School Street behind the Co-op. He boozed in the Joan Street Club and was a good domino player. Davy Warton was the manager. The Irishman came in and picked him up. They were big strong lads who had built the Kielder dam."

Matty met his wife Doreen (Ivinson) who was born in Frank Street. She went to the Majestic Cinema to watch romantic films with her friends. "Me and my mates liked the westerns. Sometimes there were beauty competitions and my wife, her sister and their friends entered, they never won and we all used to take the mickey. Every time I saw her she'd say "Have yi got a tab?" I called her Tab Hunter after the screen actor who was popular at the time.

Matty may never have met Doreen – he was evacuated during the war in 1939 to a place called Middleton, between Sedbergh and Kirby Lonsdale. "I didn't bother coming home, I left school down there when I was fourteen during the Christmas holidays and started work on the fells on New Year's Day for £1 per week. When I had asthma and bronchitis they used to put goose grease on me. My job was to chop bracken, the arches of my feet collapsed because of the nature of the job and I came back home on crutches. Then I went to work for John Spencer and Son at Newburn where the tip is now. I was responsible for driving the steam hammer. The blacksmith put the spillings under the hammer. He used to say "You're a hillbilly, get the straw oot o' yer ear." This was because after living away for a while, my accent had changed. I still go to visit the families I met there – they are in their 80s now."

Matty enjoys working on his allotment which is behind Fenham Library. He's in partnership with John Laidlaw who lives next door to him. He is still active and enjoys working on building projects in his home and garden.

Park Road showing the demolition team going in. The building to the left was the Wesleyan Methodist Church.

A Happy Childhood
by June Errington (née Wilson)

June (née Wilson) Errington was born at No 8 Clumber Street in Elswick. The Gladstone Pub was on one side and the Rifle across the road. Her mother Norah (née Lockey) married Tom Wilson. Brother Tom was the first child born in the family, then followed by June, Gordon, Sandra, Jeff, Peter and Doug. "I went to St Michael's Infant School in Brunel Street. I first got put into the "corner" with a boy called Michael Keenan for swinging the blackboard around. We were about five years old. My favourite teacher back then was Mrs McLoughlin who used to send me to the shop at playtime for a quarter of Merry Maids chocolate toffees. The first time she sent me, I took one out and put it down my sock in case she didn't give me one. However, she did and I felt very guilty. I was about seven years old."

Teachers that she remembers were Miss Birkett, headmistress (who also taught June's mother), Miss McGee, Mrs Hamilton, Miss Ayres, Miss Mckie, Mrs Dickinson and Mrs McLoughlin. I used to go to Endean's general dealers shop to buy Midget Gems, Love Hearts and Flying Saucers. When the bread van came up the street, we all loved running after it."

She attended St Michael's school until she was seven years old then

This photo was taken by Jimmy Forsyth. June is in the back yard of St Michael's Church on the day of her first communion. Also included are: Elizabeth Robb, Barbara Douglas, Theresa Macalhone, Mary McGargle.

went to Bentinck Road. The girls stayed on until they were fifteen, but the boys left there once they were eleven when they were sent to St Alyoisius. Her brother Tom caught the number 8 bus on Scotswood Road near the Low Elswick Post Office. "The senior girls worked in the upstairs rooms of the building until they reached fourteen, then spent the last year in the prefab. I loved reading and writing, playing hockey and rounders. We used the pitch at Cowgate for our games practise. I remember one day, when I was thirteen, the teacher wanted the girls to make the tea for afternoon break. Monica Kelly and myself were chosen. We went to the cookery room and Monica asked me how many tea bags to put into the tea pot and I said 13. She said "Are you sure?" Later in the day another teacher asked who had made the tea and Monica put her hand

The Rifle pub which stood on Scotswood Road.

up. The teacher said that it was like treacle. We never got picked to do that job again."

June also enjoyed attending Westmorland Road play centre after she finished school. "It was a bit like the after school clubs we have now. We watched the old silent films, Laurel and Hardy and cartoons. They were all shown in black and white. We made models with plaster, painted on them and drew pictures. Everything we did made happy times for us. I loved playing tennis in Elswick top park. In the winter we used to sledge down the bank in the lower park on Scotswood Road, whizzing between the swings – very daring! St Stephen's Church was nearby, so we were usually in the right place ready for the "Hoy oot". There were always lots of weddings."

June recalls that "Every meal was a dinner." It was a treat if she was allowed to stay for school dinners. As No 8 was right near the bottom of Clumber Street she usually went home at lunch time, except for one winter when the snow was really bad. "In the winter we had to wear wellies. It didn't matter how many pairs of socks I wore, I always had those horrible red lines around my legs. It seemed to me that I was always wearing a duffle coat! One Christmas, I remember there was really deep snow. I got a little

A Jubilee Party held on Park Road in 1977. June can be seen wearing a Union Jack hat and grey jumper.

mangle and a doll which wore a turban and a red spotty frock. The mangle had a lovely round handle with a metal wheel. When I'd had my use out of it, Dad used it to fix our Tom's toy car when the steering wheel broke. Just around the corner, in the back lane from the Gladstone was a little garage. They welded the wheel on. That car was amazing, it was red and cream with a number nine on it. Dad had an accident at work and received compensation. He took Tom to Fenwick's and said "Right, pick whatever you like." He chose this huge racing car. Dad used to push him around the streets in it with me alongside, I was two at the time."

A shopkeeper from Blundell's offered to buy the car from the Wilsons, but they refused. He wanted to put an engine inside it. Even when it wasn't used some years later, it stood in the corner of the bedroom in perfect condition even after much use. June's sister eventually took the car with her to her home. It was kept in the garden and someone stole it.

June's dad was an ashphalter. "I remember on one occasion I was sent up to Mill Lane to the company he worked for at the time, Alco – Alston Lime Company. That wouldn't be allowed nowadays."

It was also at the age of seven when June made her first Holy Communion. "I remember a man taking photos on the day. I didn't give it much thought until about seven years later when I was in Elswick Library where I saw the photos on display. I recognised myself on two photos. One where I'm in the group of girls wearing our veils and an individual picture of me standing near the wall of the church."

June could remember some of the girls taken in the group photo: Theresa McAlone. Christine McGregor and Mary McGargle. "I was 54 when I saw those photos again. Jimmy Forsyth came to the school where I've worked for twenty four years. I got talking to him and told him my story. Imagine my surprise when he remembered the photographs and said that he still had the negatives!"

Outside the Lead Works on Scotswood Road – Angus Errington is second left.

Jimmy brought the two photographs to June at the school two weeks later. "I shed some tears that day." June remembers seeing Jimmy in and around Elswick. When she was older, around 35 years old, she was laying flowers on a family grave and Jimmy was taking snaps of the gravestones.

June loved helping her mam to bake. "We were always making stuff, apple tarts, jam tarts. One day I pressed my finger into a jam tart that had just come out of the oven. I screamed, it was red hot and my finger came up like a pudding, it was really swollen. I had probably intended to lick my finger, but I never got that far. Mam took me to Mr Hay who ran the chemist shop on Scotswood Road."

The family moved to Noble Street flats. June remembers. "It had four bedrooms, bathroom, separate toilet and kitchen. It was like a palace as we had moved from a flat with one bedroom, sitting room, outside toilet and coal house on Clumber Street. When we walked onto Scotswood Road to catch the bus, we walked over the crumbling buildings. The bus stop was outside the old Armstrong's training building."

June's first job was for British Rail. She helped to make the large protective covers that were placed over the trains. She used an industrial sewing machine which operated with double needles. "A girl that lived on my block had a job there, she got me an interview. The twine had to be stitched double through the fabric. We had to push it under the presser foot. One day, I kept my hand under a little longer than usual and it came down on my finger. It swelled up and went all black. The doctor had to force a needle through my nail to let the blood out."

June met Angus Errington in 1972 and was married at Newcastle Civic Centre. Their first home was in Helen Street above a shop. Angus was working for the lead works on Scotswood Road. They now live on Benwell Lane where Angus has an allotment.

After two years, June was made redundant when the company closed down. She worked for Jackson the Tailor at Old Fold in Gateshead. She was there for 22 years before moving on to Rowntree's at Fawdon. Her daughter Lynn was born in September 1975. June's son, Lee, was born in 1980. June now works at St John's School on Armstrong Road. St John's replaced the old South Benwell School which was on Atkinson Road."

"Things are very comfortable for folks today. My Dad is 86 now, he was born in Elswick East Terrace. He often says "I remember when it was a no shoe time.""

Elswick East Terrace in 1967.

Taking the Bottles Back
by Nancy Shields (née Nichol)

Nancy was born at 24 Maria Street in 1949, she had two brothers Joe and Jimmy. Her dad Jimmy worked at Vickers and mam Florrie had worked in a paint factory and also at various pubs along Scotswood Road. "I must have been in every pub along that road, the Delaval Arms, Hydraulic, the Gun, the Globe, the Fountain and all the others."

Nancy was often called on to carry out errands and jobs for people in the area. "I remember going to Mrs Young's on a Sunday, she lived in Greenhow Place next to Maria Street. She lived in the bedroom in the front of the flat and her son Raymond and his wife were in the other room. I was sent to fetch her Sunday papers. She always gave me two and sixpence, which was a lot of money then. I used to sit on her chair and talk to her. I used to jump over the wall of the shop to take bottles when nobody was looking. I took them into the shop to claim the three pence back from each one. If anyone bought a bottle of pop from the bar they would take one out of the crate and stamp it with their own mark. So they were paying for it twice. Mam sent me to collect the family allowance, she had the price and change worked out to the penny, but if she sent our Jimmy, she didn't get any change back."

Florrie Nichol wearing a fabulous hat.

One day a neighbour knocked on the door at No 24 to voice her suspicions that Jimmy had been stealing milk tokens from the front door steps around the streets. "No, it's not our Jimmy!" replied Mrs Nichol. Then she went indoors to check his room. She found the tokens and made him take every one of them back. Nancy knew that her mother would never admit to anyone else that Jimmy was in the wrong.

Nancy and her brother Jimmy also had paper rounds from Reggie Moore's corner shop. "We used to collect the paper delivery money in a leather satchel. Sometimes the customers would say "Can I pay you double next week. We went every Saturday and Sunday morning and after school. I had to write down everything that was paid. We used to get a good tip or a nice present from the old ladies. I remember when Mr Welch was campaigning to become a councillor, I delivered leaflets for him through all of the front doors."

"I remember going to the Co-op for mam to buy a quarter of butter. They used a big knife to cut a slab from a huge mountain of butter. I loved to watch them cutting it, it looked like a wedding cake with discs of butter piled one on top of the other. Bella Booth's shop was on the other side of Buddle Road, when I went into the shop she would say "Guard that door till I go to the toilet." The toilet was a bucket in the corner of the shop with a curtain around it."

Nancy remembered that her dad owned a pigeon loft at the Panyards on top of a hill. "Dad used to ask our Joe to go and clean them out, but he had to offer him a shilling to carry out the work. I used to go all the time but dad would say "You can't wear that flairy frock, go

Nancy at the Benwell Reunion at the West Denton Fire Station Club in 2007.

and get something proper on!" I loved to shake the tin with seeds in and when they came back after a race I clocked them in. Our Jimmy had a hen, he got it when it was a baby chicken and called it Jiffy after the show Jiffy the Broomstick Man."

Nancy recalled that there was a fish shop facing the Hydraulic Crane pub on Scotswood Road. "If we took newspapers to the owner, we were given a free bag of chips. Back then they wrapped the food up in old newspapers. I loved me mam's pea and ham soup, but sometimes I'd hear her complaining to Tommy Wilson's mam Gladys who lived at number 26. "Look here Gladie, I've made all of these lovely pies and they're eating crisp sandwiches!!"

Gladys answered "Send them down here."

A shopkeeper that Nancy remembers was Paul Bahanda who's family ran the general dealers shop on Buddle Road. "Paul became a good friend. His dad had opened the shop which used to be the old Co-op. When they first came they had a battle at first. Kids used to ask them for tartan thread and striped paint. But they quickly became popular people in the community. Paul had a motorbike and he used to let us sit on it.

When Nancy was younger she went along to Rye Hill where her mother worked. "We got the bus back, and mam's brother, Dondie Brewer, would be on the bus sometimes after playing at one of the pubs in town. He always had his banjo with him and had the bus jumping all the way home. He was a fantastic player. He lived across the road from my nana. My mam worked at the Cushie Butterfield, the Old Hall Social Club and the Joan Street Club, but she ended her working days on the bread and cakes stand at Woolworths."

The building known locally as The Havelock where the first meetings of the Elswick Local History Group first took place. Nancy was a regular at the social club here.

Nancy smiled as she remembered sitting on the cellar steps outside Reggie Moore's shop. "We used to wait for Peter Moore to let us into the cellar when he was practising with his band the Bluebeats. Some of the band members were Dave Anderson, Joe May, Pete Mickelson and Bob Barton. I loved listening to the Beatles songs. Bob later went on to sing and play with the band Beckett, they were on *The Old Grey Whistle Test* on television. Some of my mates who also hung around there were Olive Bonner, Sylvia Hall and her boyfriend Roy (who she later married), Linda Liddle, Lilian Erskine and Yvonne Luscombe."

"We sometimes went to the Moorside Club at the bottom of Atkinson Road opposite South Benwell School, it was a prefab. May Sterling ran it and there was a tuck shop, dancing, table tennis and records playing. We also went to the Grainger Park Boys'

Club on Scotswood Road at the Elswick end. There was a boxing ring in the basement where Paddy Power practised and one of the Prendergast lads played football. The Power family ran the Forge Hammer pub at the bottom of Edgeware Road. I went around with their daughter Fran."

Jobs that Nancy held began with her first position as a machinist at Levine's clothing factory. "I made trousers, skirts, blouses, culotte dresses and suits. I made buttons and covered them with fabric, all done on the machine. It was really noisy in there, but the lasses were fantastic – we had a good working relationship with everyone there. I remember wearing a white pleated skirt – they were popular. I made my own jeans with bell bottoms and tartan pieces sewn on the outside lower hem and a blouse also with bell sleeves. I wore them with nice shoes and a leather or suede coat – they were in fashion in the '60s. I always wanted a long navy suede coat with a leather collar. We either went to the Crown or Savoy cinemas and went dancing to the majestic in town. I saw the Animals at the Downbeat."

When Nancy worked at the paint factory, her brothers Joe and Jimmy and her mother were already employed there. Joe also worked as a pitman in a local mine for a while. "The building stood just before you go over the bridge at Shieldfield. I didn't stay there for long, then I went back into sewing. I worked at J & J Fashions on Scotswood Road for a while and then moved on to cooking at nursing homes, then I retired."

Nancy was a popular member of the community and lived in Benwell all her life and helped to run various clubs. She went to the Havelock in Elswick where she always took a buffet on her birthday. "We would go to the Catholic Club in the cellar of St Joseph's Church on Armstrong Road. Carol, my friend served behind the bar. I used to take the kids there – they enjoyed the line dancing. We took a buffet with us."

She cooked at the Ferguson's Lane Club when they held events. I was present at the Christmas lunch, all of the members are looked after, all received a present, money which had been saved up over the year and a dinner fit for a king, followed by a choice of puddings and coffee and chocolates. The groups run pie and pea suppers and many fundraising activities. There are bingo, raffle prizes, domino card games a friendly atmosphere with people that she knew for years.

Sadly since this interview Nancy became ill but still carried on helping friends and neighbours. Nancy was married to her partner Alan Shields at the Freeman Hospital on the Bobby Robson Cancer Care Ward on 11th June surrounded by her family and friends. Alan had obtained a special license for the ceremony. It must have been the only buffet that Nancy did not prepare herself. She died on 15th June 2010 and is big miss to everyone who knew her.

Left: This photo was taken on a night out when we all went along to the Fairholm Club on Ferguson's Lane. From left to right: Joe Jocker, Alan Shields, Audrey Chisholm and Nancy.

In The Pink
by Pat Horsefield

Pat was born in 1947 at Amelia Street. She was christened at St Michael's Church. She says: "Father Crombie was the priest who carried out the ceremony. His brother works at St John Vianney on Chapel House."

Pat also attended St Michael's School. "It was a very tiny school attached to the church. There weren't very many children. I remember the crayons. We used thick and thin ones. One lad in my class shuved one of the thick ones up my nose and it got stuck up my left nostril. I went to hospital to have it cauterised. They packed my nose with horrible yellow gauze. I could hear the hairs burning. That memory has stuck with me and I still have trouble with my nose now. I do remember the teachers – Sister Sebastian and Sister Michael, who was very young and everyone admired her. Then there were Miss Humble and Mrs Larkin."

Pat's first communion at St Bede's Church, Whickham View.

Pat's dad, was born at Shields, he worked as a telephone engineer, putting up telegraph poles. "He came into the house with dead animals that had flown or run into the lorry." Her mam worked at Carricks and for the Station Hotel in Newcastle. She also lived at No 3 Amelia Street and her Uncle Robbie and Auntie Joan lived at No 5. He worked for the bus service, on the trolley's. He was also a fire fighter. Joan worked at St James' Park on the catering side.

"My uncle Robbie drove the charabancs to Cullercoats or Whitley Bay. We went on the trips. Everybody baked, got pots of tea and made sandwiches. We called them soggies, they were always egg and tomato. To this day I can't stand egg and tomato sandwiches. There were always mussels and wiliks, my nana called them snots. They were served in a white paper bag with a pin in the corner. Chips, they always tasted different near the sea."

Pat played knocky nine door like most kids. She loved playing Cowboys and Indians until a lad who was carrying a toy gun hit her with the butt: "Meggie

Pat's uncle Robbie standing near the charabanc which he drove on trips.

Mcgarry came around the corner with her shopping. She ran across the street to chase him and dropped the bags. There were oranges all over the place." She still has the scar above her left eyebrow. On another occasion Pat tells of a railway transporter that hit a bus and broke her nose.

Pat remembered her granddad: "I used to go down to the back entrance of the lane to the pub down really steep wooden steps. It was on the other corner to the Crown pub. I went with some money to ask for a jug of beer for granddad. It was always on a Saturday or Sunday."

Pat's mam went down a little lane to take rags to get a little money. Pat remembers at Easter and Christmas that there would always be new clippy mats. "At Easter we always got new sandals and ankle socks. There were no chocolate eggs, only paste ones which were stained. Aunt Joan used to use onion skins and they went a lovely mottled colour like brindle dogs – blacks and creams. She used to put elastic bands around them before they went into the dye and that created a striped effect. On a Sunday morning, coming home from church, there would be the smell of stottie cake – Granny Casey would be cooking. I looked forward to the smell as I came through the front door. There were steep stairs up to the sitting room and the bedroom."

Maggie and Tom, cousins of Pat, sitting on their chair in the back yard. Notice the proggy mats over the bannister.

Moira (Pat's younger sister) and Pat pose with the car. It's parked on Amelia Street near the Rock pub.

"The kitchen was tiny. Three steps down to the kitchen and mountains of stairs to the back yard. There were around twenty to twenty five of them. Half a dozen wooden, then the rest were concrete with a wooden bannister at Amelia Street. The yard was quite high, sort of raised. One day I was coming up the stairs from the outside toilet and a dish of water was thrown down. I was drenched. We laugh about it now. People threw the used water out so that the stairs got a wash too."

Pat recalls how the women were out every day to donkey stone the step or hanging out of the sash windows cleaning the glass. "I got the job of putting newspaper on a string for the netty, wringing the mangle while mam put the clothes through. But, one job I really hated was when I had to black lead the oven. I remember those hot water bottles which were made of China. We put water through the round neck and put the stopper back in. We had to put a blanket around it. When it came out of the oven dad wrapped the hot blanket around us while mam put the bottle into the bed. Your pillow was warm and your feet warm and in the winter the mat was on the bed."

She laughs as she thinks about when the

20

streets were thick with snow. "It was brilliant for sledging. We had someone to keep watch on us because sometimes we carried on over the Scotswood Road causing havoc among the traffic. The toot checked to see if anything was coming along the road. Another time when a toot was needed was when the men played flip halfpenny. We would watch to see if a policeman was approaching."

Her mother was born in 1917 on 2nd September, she is 93 years of age. She was married at St Mary's Church in town. "She used to knit, crochet, embroider and make clothing on an old treadle machine, she made some beautifully embroidered cards. The new fangled electric ones are not the same. She made me a trouser suit. My daughter said Mam, ladies don't wear trousers. That was forty years ago."

Pat's Auntie Mary played an important role in her life. "When she was about twenty years old I used to watch her riding on her bike with the lads. They were always doing off somewhere to smoke cigarettes. She used to wear ankle socks. I idolised her. I used to pull my hair up and roll stockings around then fan my hair over the top like a doughnut. I used sugar and water as hairspray, it attracted the wasps, one thing I hated. I used to pull out old shirts to make little sun dresses."

Elswick Park Archway can be seen in the background. Pat and her aunt Mary are enjoying the sunshine.

Pat worked on the Arc Project for St James' Church making a pair of caterpillars, ladybirds and Mrs Ham (Noah's daughter-in-law). She meets her fellow knitters at Cornerstone on Tuesdays and Thursdays every week.

Below: A letter home from Pat's Uncle Billy who was serving in the army during the First World War:

April 5/4/17

Dear Sis,

A few lines in answer to your letter and cigs received yesterday. Many thanks, they were like a godsend. You see we are not exactly in a position to carry any hereabouts and when we are gasping for a smoke, there is nothing like a good old Woodbine.

Well Sis, I'm still in the pink and glad to hear all's well again at the factory. But I see it's not the case at home. Mother tells me the pit is just working 3 to 4 days a week so I guess they will be feeling the pinch now. So I've told them not to send cigs and things. Soon we will all get back together again.

No doubt you'll see the papers about the games out here so you'll see good reasons for good hopes for the end of all our troubles. "No chance" there, I bet there will be some stiff times ahead of us yet, but if the luck still holds for us all we'll see us all in blighty before many months are over. Then you bet, I'll have a canny time to make up for lost times. All our prayers.

With love to all, love and affection, Billy. Write soon, don't forget cigs are thankfully received anytime.

Truly
Billy

A Family of Watchmakers
by Ronnie and Warren Clarke

Ronnie Clarke was born in 1943 at Colston Street. He attended Canning Street School, passed his 11 + exams and went to Pendower School. He later married Rene. "My son Warren was born in 1964 at 82 Condercum Road opposite Custombilt. Young Ronnie was born in 1962."

"My first job was for Dean Motor Company, I was an apprentice repair man at a showroom at the Haymarket area of town. Next I took a job as an apprentice watchmaker for David Summerfield in Northumberland Street – I served my time there. I worked for myself after that at a workshop in Percy Street. I bought my first corner shop at the junction of Colston Street and Dolphin Street, it was a general dealers, that was about 1965. That business was sold and I opened the Adelaide Toy Shop, the building was where Search is now. My mother Gladys and dad Arthur served in the shop. We sold fancy goods. People could put things away. I used to say "There's two and sixpence off, there you are."

Warren and his pals line up outside Bond Street Baths. Canning Street School is in the background.

Ronnie and the family moved further along Adelaide Terrace to where they own Specials. Warren remembers. "We opened Specials at numbers 58-62. This shop was once split into two, Alex Cooper's clothing shop and Clarke's hardware in the other. There were two three bedroomed flats above. I remember when granddad discovered an unexploded bomb. All of these shops have cellars and he noticed the bomb bedded into the foundations of the wall. The bomb disposal team was called out. Malcolm's sold riding boots on the other side of the road to this building. I also remember when my granny Gladys was working for Custombilt, she washed cars. Someone stole a car and rode it right through the front plate glass window. The driver broke his nose."

"I loved going to Bond Street baths when I was a kid, I have a photo of me and my pals all lined up."

Canning Street School children enjoying a drink of milk. Ronnie Clark is pictured at the back of the room drinking his milk with a straw. He is wearing a grey jumper with navy blue and red stripes

Warren attended Canning Street School in 1969. "I remember being sent to Mr Winter in the head master's office when I broke the tin world globe. We had been carrying on. I was surprised that I didn't get the belt, I offered to pay for it. He just said "Well, are you pleased with yourself? There's no need to pay, just behave yourself in future!"

Warren enjoyed playing football in the lane when he was a kid. "We used the back doors as goal. When we weren't playing football there might be a wooden frame with wire mesh lying around from the building sites. We discovered that when we jumped on the wire it was like a trampoline. One day we were playing near the Conhope Lane. There was a yard and a shed, and me and my pals were on a small wall nearby. I climbed onto the high roof and as I was waving to my mates, the roof caved in and I fell banging my head against a tipper wagon. I was sent to hospital. When we weren't playing around the doors we caught a single decker red bus on the West Road to Heddon on the Wall. We would be there all day. Sometimes we went to Crawcrook looking for newts. I loved bonfire night, there'd be up to five bonfires in one lane, all blazing away together. I always went to my Aunt Meg's house, she baked the most lovely cakes. I'd run along there hers and my dad would play war because he wanted to be away to the Pendower Club and I was never back home in time."

"My first job was as an apprentice watchmaker for Northern Goldsmiths. The lads knew that I was only young, so they were always playing jokes on me until I cottoned on. When they asked me to ask at the stores for a long stand, I didn't click at first because some of the clocks had long pendulums. Then, the store man said "Right lad, you've stood there long enough." I did click when they asked me to go for bubbles for the spirit level and nail holes. I remember one day when they asked me if I had seen the golden rivet. You know the statue of the lady on the clock outside? There was a dome, a kind of bell tower inside. By the clockmaker's workshop

Specials shop on Adelaide Terrace. From left to right: Davy Kell, Carol (née James) Allen, Warren Clarke, Ronnie Clark (Snr) and Anne Milor who has been manager there for fourteen years.

there was a big wooden door and they showed me inside to look at this rivet. Once inside they closed the door and I climbed in. It was approaching 12 o'clock and the first chime had just clicked in, the noise was deafening. I was only 16 years old. I shouted "Let is oot!"

Warren only had to suffer one chime and his workmates released him. He worked for the company for five years until he was made redundant. "There are five generations of watchmakers in our family. It started with my grandfather Arthur. He was self taught, people brought their watches and clocks to him if they were too fast or slow. He worked from his living room and he used to say "There's a ticket for you." Then the customers would collect their things later. Arthur Clarke was his first son, who later served his time with Reid and Sons. He owned a jewellers on Adelaide Terrace for 40 years, only retiring in 2008. I remember when we all lived together, us in the bottom flat, granddad in the middle and my uncle Arthur on top in Condercum Road. I still know our dividend number 25889."

Warren has two children, Reece and Jasmine from his relationship with Tracey and two children, Olivia and Ellie together with his partner Nicola – and step daughter Abbey.

Tents, Nets and Pigeons
by Tom Luscombe

Tom Luscombe was born at 20 Ramshaw Street, Elswick in 1925, His father was Charles Reginald and mother Mary Ann. His brothers and sisters were Norman, George, Beatrice, Doris, Charles, Alfie, Kenneth and Margaret. "We had the downstairs flat. There were 2 bedrooms, a sitting room and a small scullery. The scullery had a mangle with a heavy roller for squeezing water out. I used to turn the handle. We had an iron which hot coals were put inside and the shutter pulled up. We had an old poss tub for the washing. In the living room, mam used to put the clothes on a washing line across the room as many families did in those days. The heat from the coal fire dried them.

End of the shift. Water Street where Tom listened to the sound of the hob nailed boots on the cobbles as the men finished at the end of the day at Elswick Works at the bottom of Rendle Street.

One of his first memories include going to Elswick Low Park. "We used to get in from a side gate. I used to go there to watch the older blokes playing bowls. We played on the swings and the shuggy boat, it was a kind of seesaw shape which went back and forward instead of up and down. I remember there was a maypole there too. I used to lie on the grass and look up to St Stephen's Church steeple. All that's left is the steeple now, the church was demolished.

The top park was across Westmorland Road and we called it the posh one. There was a little shop, it looked like a Hansel and Gretel house where they sold tea and coffee. There were greenhouses, tennis courts, fountains and we climbed a set of rocks

Elswick Low Park. Jimmy Forsyth took this photo of the Beveridge children playing. He was befriended by the family after his accident at ICI where his eye was damaged.

which we called "The Mountains". When I look at them now, they're not that big, but as kids, to us they seemed huge. Kids enjoyed going down the shute, a kind of slide. The park had caged birds and animals, it was very interesting. The Savoy cinema was on the other corner. A Walt Disney film, *Snow White and the Seven Dwarves* was the first I ever saw, I was captivated. I went to see it with a couple of mates – Ernie Summerville was one of them."

Alexander Street Boys' club was one of Tom's haunts. It was run by Mr Teasdale who lived on Bentinck Road. Tom said that it kept them off the streets. Activities included boxing, Ludo, Snakes and Ladders. He remembers that it cost him halfpence for a cup of OXO. He also called in to a fish shop which was near Glue House lane and Beaumont Street. He recalls seeing the pit wheel and the bridge at the bottom which continued over Scotswood Road carrying the coal wagons. It took a while after the war ended before it was pulled down. "I remember a coal man, Mr Jones, on Beaumont Street, the horse was kept in the back yard. He used to hire a bike out for half an hour. We went to school with two of his sons, one was called Billy. He used to go past St Michael's Church on Westmorland Road on his horse and cart. He paid us a couple of bob to fill the bags for him. We put the bags on the scales. It was a heavy job and the men had to wear something on their heads."

Many people relied on odd jobs to make ends meet. "My dad used to make fishermen's nets in the back yard, he had rigged up a bracket to weave them on. He also made tents to sell. Canvas was draped across the clothes line. He used a tool to press the needle through. We didn't use a coal house as he kept his pigeons in there. He cut the top plank of wood out so they could get back inside. Dad joined the pigeon union. He knew how to handle the birds, by putting his fingers under the top of their legs. I used to help by rattling seeds up in a tin to get them back down from the roof. He used to play war if they didn't come down quickly. People raced their pigeons in our street and the adjoining ones. A lorry came around, collected up all of the pigeons in baskets from our street, a number stamped on. They were taken to France and let loose at a certain time to begin the race back home. The stronger ones made for

Beaumont Street where Tom Luscombe rode his delivery bike. Not many families owned cars in those days. Today, similar streets would be edge to edge with vehicles.

Newcastle. Neighbours painted the doors of their crees a different colour so that the birds knew where to make for. Then the pigeons would be clocked in on their arrival home. There were prizes for the winners, a cup or money."

Mrs Smith was a neighbour of the Luscombe's family. She lived in Tom's back lane. Ramshaw Street and Rendle Street shared the lane. "We called her Ducky Smith because she raised ducks in her back yard. There was another lady who we called Granny Smith, she made ginger wine. If we went up to her house with a bottle, we got a halfpenny off the price. She used fresh ginger to grind down. There was a shop on the corner of Rendle Street and Sanderson. It was called Ashworth's. Smith's shop was slightly higher up. When I went up Rendle and turned left along Beaumont Street there was a house shop which was run by a man called Jow who was Jewish. He sold sugar, tea, odds and ends and books and comics. I bought the *Beano, Dandy, Film Fun, Radio Times, Hotspur* and *Wizard*."

Tom also bought sweets – caramels were his favourites. He remembered the names of some – Pegg's bar, Regent's bar and walnut whirls. "There was an Italian shopkeeper, his surname sounded like Parro, but we called him Mr Parrot, like the bird. We didn't know how to pronounce it. I remember when we had the first Italian ice cream shop, Mark Toney's. The shopkeeper was a real Italian with a huge moustache, he went around the streets with a barrow with an ice barrel in the middle shouting "Icea da creama". We used to come out with our half pennies. The Dotchin brothers lived in one of the old houses and their dad was a baker. When we went into their back yard it was all painted white. We thought it looked very posh. But it was painted like that for hygiene reasons. There was a board in the window with samples on. People bought bread there. All of the little industries were within the streets, you could get anything you wanted around the doors. There were fellas that cobbled shoes. Also a man who went around selling kippers."

Most of the cooking was done on the range oven which was integral with the fireplace. The boiler heated the water. "The fire had a grate and underneath was the fire. The grill was dropped and mam used to heat a pan of broth over it. One day we

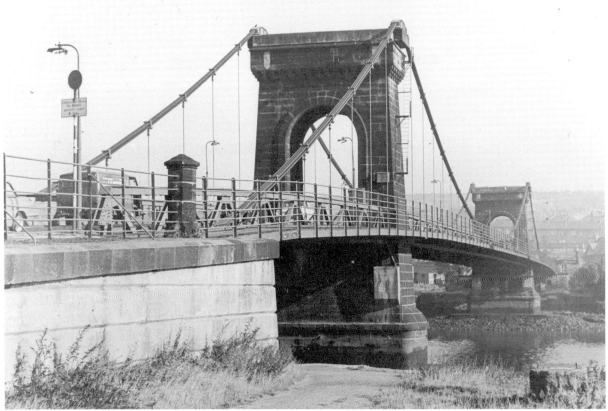

Chain Bridge. The bridge was so narrow that only one lane of traffic was allowed to pass at a time. This bridge was replaced by a box girder style a little further west from where the old one had stood.

were devastated because the kitten got in to keep warm and the door got closed. We didn't know it was in there, poor little thing. My mam was always busy, she had a hard life, she was a quiet natured woman. She used to go to a church near Diana Street and to St Aidan's on Glue House Lane."

"I was never in the house. I got to know the area really well. I'd turn out from Elswick along Scotswood Road, it was one of my routes. Me and my pals used to go bathing in the Tyne. We could get down easily by the Chain Bridge. We walked everywhere and sometimes went along to Blaydon to swim there, always walking. Sometimes it was 11 o'clock at night before we got back for a cup of tea and something to eat. We looked for new places and new adventures. There were two toll cabins on the Chain Bridge where we were supposed to pay to get through, but we always dodged it."

Tom enjoyed running along the high back yard walls. He ran the full length of the lane and sometimes going off on an angle along someone's inner wall. "One day I sat on the junction of the two walls and misjudged the distance. I fell straight down into the yard. I hurt myself but didn't break any bones."

He attended Cruddas Park School from the age of five. Tom had a love of books, at first enjoying Fairy Tales and mysteries. "One year, I was given a prize of books for my work and being good in class. The next year I won building blocks for being top of the class. I loved looking out of my window when we moved to 101 Beaumont Street. I watched the men running down the street wearing their hob nailed boots. They would go down to Water Street towards the Elswick Works at the bottom of Rendle Street."

Cruddas Park School. Notice the railings around the top of the building. Children played up there on the roof. The old police hut stands on the path and further along is the drinking fountain.

Tom's first job was for Hewett's Butchers shop on Beaumont Street. "Even in the winter I had to deliver provisions on the bike in the bitter cold. I didn't have the proper clothes for the weather. Mr Hewitt would say "Just go to Weidner Road, or just go to Ferguson's Lane," as if it was a couple of minutes away. I'd set off from the corner of Loadman Street or Strickland Street. It was freezing, so I decided halfway up that I wasn't going to go up there. So, I punctured the tyre and I went back crying. The second in command at the shop got the job to go up there with the stuff and I was given the job to repair the tyre with a puncture kit."

A couple of weeks later, Tom left that job and started work as a delivery boy for a fresh fish shop on Westgate Road. The routes were around much flatter streets. "I delivered dressed crabs and lobsters to hotels in town. If I got hungry I would take a little meat from each one. Sometimes I went as far as Swan Hunter Shipyards. Sometimes I would stand around near their canteen watching the ships and I became interested in them. It was a long ride back from there. One day I got chatting to the workmen and asked if there were any jobs going. One of the blokes said "Sure, go and see the foreman." I was lucky as I was just coming up to 16, I was just catching it."

Tom had enjoyed woodwork at school, so he was offered a choice. He could become a joiner or a carpenter. He became a ship's carpenter, preferring to be aboard the ship where he could lay decks and work on the doors to cabins. "I received the letter to start work in 1939. The first ship I ever worked on was the *Petrolicus*. We worked on all sorts of ships. There were two trawlers made for minesweepers. We had to change them back again to trawlers. We used to get big orders with so many ships being sunk by U-boats. As war progressed we had orders for air craft carriers and oil tankers. One compartment alone on a tanker would have been the whole length of the West End Library. The whole thing weighed around 200 and odd thousand tons. There were cargo ships with holding tanks to store equipment, machinery, guns and tanks."

He went off to serve in the army before returning to resume work back at the shipyards. "I had my last drink in the Hydraulic Crane before I went away. I've still got the Guinness glass that I drank from. It's got gold embellishments on the front."

In uniform having their last drink before army life. Tom Luscombe on the right.

Tom worked on the *Illustrious*, an aircraft carrier which went to the Falklands. "We worked night and day to get it ready. The *Arc Royal* was exactly the same. It was finished in 1983. I was paid off and received redundancy. I was 58 years of age and I would have stayed working there as long as I could. They kept saying to me "When are you going to take the money and go?" but I didn't want it. I wanted to work."

A favourite photo of Tom's was taken on the very top of a ship. "There were no handrails or safety harnesses and we just got on with it."

Tom still returns to the West End from his home in Walker. He sometimes calls in to the West End Library to look through the old photos stored there by the West Newcastle Picture History Collection. The Cruddas Park Flats stand over the ground where the old streets once stood, so he goes through the Elswick folders to pick out schools, shops and photos of the parks he played in as a child.

"It's good to see that some of the old street names are retained on the flats, such as The Pines after Pine Street. It's all being regenerated again with a new name, Riverside Dene, but it'll always be Cruddas Park to me."

Tom sitting on top of a ship in the Neptune Yard at Swan Hunter's Shipyard.

What Can You Buy For Five Shillings These Days?
by Ann Cusack (née Reay)

Ann Reay was born in 1940. She was brought up by her mother Martha (née Jones) and stepfather Arthur, who was known locally as Arty. He was a train driver and travelled the route to Carlisle. "He used to toot the horn when he reached Elswick Station. All of the kids waited until he waved to them. They thought it was great that their uncle was a train driver. He had been a fireman for years before he had that job."

Ann was born on Buddle Road, just opposite the gates of South Benwell School where she attended from the age of four until she was fifteen years of age. Teachers she remembered were Mr Tweddle (Headmaster), Mrs Bell, Mr Hicks who taught music and Mrs Hedley who gave cookery lessons.

Ann remembered that Arty was fond of backing a horse. "He wasn't too well one day, he asked mam to go to the betting shop to place the bet. He asked her to take the money from his trouser pocket. She then realised that she had put

Ann's dad Arty was a train driver. Children congregated near the station to watch the steam blast from the funnel.

them in the wash with the money inside, the trousers were blowing fiercely on the line. There was a roll of notes tightly rolled and very wet, a total of £360 in ten shilling and one pound notes. The money was put on the floor in front of the heater to dry out. When the family weren't looking our Yorkshire Terrier Cindy started to chew them."

She remembered some of the shops in the area. One of those was Dolly's shop on Buddle Road. "I went up there to buy one pennyworth of bruised fruit. I would cut off the bashed bits and it tasted lovely. It was one penny to buy a sour cooking apple. When I'd finished eating it I asked my pal "Do you want the gowk?" I loved bananas, I ate them more than any other fruit and people used to say that I had feet like bananas because I was spla footed."

"I often ran errands for neighbours. Mr Sanderson sent me for messages to Mr Heinzman's pork shop, he always gave me a copper for going. I always spent the money at Peacocks hardware shop where I would buy little milk and sugar bowls to keep for presents. It was funny when mam told me that she was going to buy sliced bread. I imagined that you could buy two or three slices, I didn't realise that it was a whole loaf!"

Ann's mam was an accomplished

Arty, Martha and Ann together on a night out.

needlewoman and knitter. "She put wool away at Dodgson's shop. Everyone did this back then; they selected the wool they wanted and paid for one ball at a time until the item was finished. People couldn't afford to buy the whole lot in one go. Everyone commented on how neat my mam's work was. In the late 1970s she made a patchwork bedspread and pillowcases from remnants of fabric which were left over from dresses she had made for my daughters. We lost count of the number of crotched cot blankets she made and embroideries which we still have today. Mam used to buy the templates from Bainbridge (John Lewis now). When I worked at M & S anyone who was having a baby got a blanket which my mam had made, each one beautifully ornate with scallops around the edges. She was also a good cook. I remember when we lived in Aline Street she used to bake on the marble surface, the pastry was lovely and cool."

Sylvia Wood who helped to create the Woolly West (the knitting project that created old streets and buildings in the West End) said that Ann's mam knitted the most beautiful jumpers. "One in particular I remember which had a huge welt at the bottom with a very complicated pattern. I tried everywhere to find one like it. I saw an advert in the newspaper from a man who collected old knitting patterns from different eras. When I looked at the patterns shown in the ad, there it was, so I sent him half a dozen of mine and asked if he would swap. He sent it to me and I made the jumper."

At the front, Ann is wearing a buttonhole in an oatmeal two piece suit. The occasion is the wedding of Grace Kell and Jim Taylor in 1958. The pals are standing outside the back door of Grace's house in Maughan Street. From left to right, front row: Eddie Kell, Ann and Maureen Brown. Middle: Valerie Atkinson, Pat Robson (wearing pearls) who lived at Eveline Gardens. Allan Middleton at back. Candy (peeping out). The lad wearing the grey suit was Eddie's pal.

A friend and neighbour of Ann's remembers: "The houses at the top of Helen Street were in better condition than those at the bottom. The landlord didn't carry out repairs. When any of the family went to the outside toilet during the rain, they had to sit on the toilet holding an umbrella as there was a huge hole in the roof. There were always pages from the *Radio Times* hanging on a nail."

Ann's first job was for Milburn the chemist in the Haymarket area of Newcastle. She has worked for Boots in Grainger Street, Hall Fosters (Wholesale chemists) in Temple Street near the Essoldo Cinema. Ann also worked for Bookless in town where she was in charge of the messages on wreaths for Thompson's opposite Elswick Park. She later worked for M & S for 23 years until she retired.

She met her husband Ted at the Pendower Hut dance. "On our first date Ted had to borrow ten shillings from his cousin. We went to the Rex Cinema in Benwell Village where we sat in the one and nine pence seats (the dear ones). He bought me a box of Cadbury's chocolates for one shilling and threepence and he still had five shillings left at the end of the night!"

Ted was born in Cottenham Street near the big lamp and he attended St Aloysius School. Ann remembered that Ted's family kept chickens at their house when they lived at Cowgate. Ann recalls: "Ted lived there from being two years of age until we married on 6th June 1959 at St James Church, Benwell. My dress was white in broderie anglaise. The material cost £5 and a woman from Westerhope made it. Her name was Mrs Isabelle Hill, but everyone knew her as Belle. I only weighed 6 stone 10 pounds and I was very petite. My four cousins were bridesmaids and they were dressed in nasturtium coloured garments. The reception was held at Tilly's Restaurant in Blackett

Street. There were 53 guests at ten shillings and sixpence per head with 27 glasses of whisky at two shillings and eight pence each. My mam worked at the Cochrane Street Club for 30 shillings (£1.50) a week and this paid for the wedding. The total cost of the reception came to £39 and I still have the receipts."

"When we first married we rented a flat in Aline Street. The rent was 18 shillings a week. We had our first daughter Deborah Ann and lived there for four years until we moved to Cruddas Park in a maisonette opposite the Rock pub, 14 Mulberry Place, the rent was three pounds sixteen shillings. We loved the house, but hated the entrance. Our second daughter Jane Louise was born there on New Year's Eve, 1968. Whilst living in Cruddas Park we found the neighbours to be very close and friendly and would do anything to help each other. Nothing was a bother."

Ann's mam Martha had been talking to her neighbour Mrs Goodwin who wanted an exchange for a smaller house. Iris Steadman was on the council for Cruddas Park and when she found out that we wanted an exchange, she submitted a reference for them. In later years, Martha was presented with a key from Jeremy Beecham as being the first resident who lived at River View Lodge.

Ted became a contract joiner for Saddler Brothers at Benton Industrial Estate. "I got £7 per week from Ted which was a lot of money back then. I did the shopping at Laws Stores on the corner of Clara Street and Adelaide Terrace. There was always a smell of

Ann and Ted's first fancy dress party. Looking very grand dressed as vicar and nun. Ted stepped from the house first and neighbours didn't recognise him – they feared that something had happened to Ann. When she came out next dressed as a nun they burst out laughing.

paraffin and moth balls. There were mops and dishcloths all over the place, I wondered how the owner ever found anything. We lived at the house in Dobson Close for fifteen years and became firm friends with our neighbours Teresa and Eddie Warwick who lived next door. During the 1960s we campaigned with other residents for a swimming pool at Elswick. We have now been friends for over forty years and share man holidays both at home and abroad with them. They still pop around every week to our two bedroom semi at Denton Burn where we have lived for the last twenty four years."

Aschem Chemists on Whickham View – Arthur Melton and Ann Cusack. Arthur was born at Elm Street.

Ann and Ted have attended many events and functions. Ann laughs as she looks through her photos and she remembers a Halloween fancy dress party.

"Ted stepped from the house first. He was dressed as a vicar. A neighbour across the road was concerned that something had happened to me, until she saw me come out next wearing a nun's habit. She fell about laughing."

Ann and Ted's daughters both live close by in Denton Burn and they see them and their four grandchildren every day.

Trains on One Side and Buses on the Other
by Dennis Carss

Dennis Carss was born in 1934 at the Princess Mary Hospital. At the time, his family lived at Juliet Street. Dennis was brought up as an only child by his Grandfather Matthew and Grandmother Ada. Matthew worked as a slinger at Vickers which involved connecting the hook of the crane to the object which was ready to be lifted. He had formerly worked as a blacksmith's striker. Between 1937 and 1939 they lived at 44 Meldon Street. "I remember standing in the street on Sunday, 3rd September 1939 when war was declared – everyone was standing in the street talking about it. I started at Bentinck Road School the next day. The playground was laid out to look like streets with Belisha Beacons (zebra crossings). I remember that there were lots of toy cars and children pedalling around in them."

Later in 1939 the family moved to 67 St John's Road which was south of Armstrong Road. The shop next door was run by the Williams family. "It was a purpose built shop – not one of those conversions from the front room."

Dennis attended Elswick Road School from five years of age until he was ten. One teacher he remembers was Miss Pearson. He received a card from her with Tom Tom the Piper's Son on the front when he was absent from school with whooping cough. "I still have that card. I don't remember much about the building as in those days you were in the same classroom for all lessons. Not like today where the children move around. I remember Miss Gatoff, a Jewish lady."

"In 1945 we moved back to Meldon Street (this time No 33), I remember Leonard Capoldi who lived across the road. His greatest

Elswick Road School in 1984.

claim to fame was when he went along the street to Green's Electrical Shop. He was carrying an accumulator to have it charged when he dropped it. There were acid burns on the pavement for years. An accumulator was a glass cased battery filled with acid. When charged it provided power for about one week. Two doors up from us lived Miss Bell, an usherette who worked in the kiosk at the Brighton Cinema. There was also a Co-op on Bentinck Crescent which our family used. I can still remember the check number – 63917."

At Westgate Hill school I was placed into Mrs Walton's scholarship class, which I had no idea at the time what that meant. Mrs Walton came into the classroom one day and announced that two of us had passed for Royal Grammar and six of us had passed for Rutherford Grammar School. The Butler Education Act of 1944 created free education for secondary schools and also the 11 + exam. My grandparents provided the school uniform. I was asked to provide my birth certificate. For the first time I was made aware that the lady who I thought was my older sister was my mother."

He didn't own a pair of shoes until he was sixteen years old. Before that Dennis only wore hob nailed boots. "They came in very useful at Rutherford Grammar as the building had concrete floors. This made for excellent sliding areas. My friend Billy's mother used to buy him a new uniform every year, so she gave me his old one – which was still in good condition. Initially at the school it was staffed with a mixture of older masters some of whom had been brought out of retirement to teach us until the end of the war. The demobbed teachers came back gradually to resume their old jobs."

"Rutherford School for Boys, by then Rutherford Grammar School, was at Bath Lane. Charles Stewart Hall was head. The form master in later years was Maurice Heslop. Mr Hindson for physics. Mr Carmichael taught us to play chess. He sat in the library facing the wall with five boys behind him who were all playing against him at the same time. Basil Quinn taught maths. My favourite subjects were chemistry, maths and physics. History wasn't my strong point. Mr Shieff the history master taught me to believe in miracles – he said to me "If you pass in history it'll be a miracle!" I did."

"I mainly went to Elswick Park with my friends. Marbles – liggies – was a favourite of ours. We gouged three holes out of the ground to aim the marbles at. Long before the days of tin foil tops, bottles had a recess at the top with about a one and a half inch disc of waxed card pressed into the recess. A smaller hole was impressed in the centre which could be pressed out with the thumb to allow the milk to be poured. We used to throw milk bottle tops at the wall and the closest to it won the tops. We also used the bottle tops to make pom-poms. We used two of them to wind the wool around. Sweets, during the war were scarce and rationed, but we did get swizzles. They came in a cellophane tube; they were little round discs of solid sherbet. I recall cutting the sweet ration coupons out of the book to keep them safe. I never did find them."

"My Gran made steamed puddings that used to hang in a linen lump on the back of the door. She also made broth, but I don't remember any big cuts of meat. One of my favourites was egg beaten in milk. I drank it from a glass. I don't suppose that would be allowed today as we are very conscious of causing illness. People enjoyed eating bread and butter with sugar on top."

"I started going to church at around eleven or twelve years of age – my grandparents weren't religious. I went along to the St Paul's choir with a friend. When I first went to join the choir the choirmaster said "You've got a cold, come back next week." I went back the next week and he told me that I couldn't sing, so I

Elswick Road Methodist Church which was on the site of the Mosque on Malvern Street.

wasn't allowed to take part. Elswick Road Methodists didn't have a choir, or voice tests, so I joined the Sunday School there. Fred Yellow was re-starting the Boys' Brigade after the war – he was a Methodist Lay Preacher. The first time I'd stayed away from home, I was about thirteen, we went to Boys' Brigade Camp at Catton. I attended the Boys' Brigade twice a week and went to bible class on Sundays. The building stood on Malvern Street; there's a mosque there now. There were three huge halls in there – one of them was used by young mothers as a welfare building where babies were weighed and checked. During the war the Ashfield Girls' Club met there. The group leader had a little Austin car and I can still remember the registration – HTN 168."

"The Savoy Cinema was at the bottom of Beechgrove Road, I remember watching the newsreel reporting the Belsen Concentration Camp liberation. I saw *The Outlaw* there starring Jane Russell, it was in black and white; it was about 1949".

The Savoy cinema where many Elswick residents watched films of the day.

When the time came for Dennis to leave school he didn't get any advice from anyone. He had no idea which kind of job to go for – so when a form was put in front of him, he wrote electrical engineer. "I never did become one. I was offered a craft opportunity with Reyrolle's. Big companies used to trawl around the schools looking for suitable people. In September 1950 I started on a pre-apprentice course at Gateshead College. In January 1951 I was in the training school at Hebburn and was trained in a range of skills; this was followed by a year working in various sections of the works connected with assembly of switch gear etc. At eighteen I chose to be a tool maker. This was a top profession in those days, very specialised. It involved working with a wide range of machine tools and further training the use of hand tools."

Dennis completed his national service with the Royal Air Force between 1955 and 1957. He returned to his old job at Cam Design which was designing cams for automatic lathes. "The cams were funny shaped metal discs which when they rotated in the lathes pushed the tool slides at precise times to machine the metal components. During my apprenticeship I had been disinclined to go to evening classes three nights a week – the Boys' Brigade and girls seeming a better use of my spare time. As a result I had no formal qualifications and in 1957 seemed I had missed out. I found that my engineering background and experience enabled me to enrol on the last year of the City and Guilds. One of the lecturers on the course, Mr McAlpine, offered me a job at Burgess Microswitches for £1000 a year; I had been head hunted!"

"While working there I gained my Higher National Certificate, then I applied to teach. I went for the interview at Newcastle College which was called Charles Trevelyan at the time. I got the job and taught there for 26 years. I taught engineering workshop technology, maths and science; later computers were to have a place in engineering and I ended up teaching computer aided drafting, programming and operating CNC (computer numerically controlled) machine tools, word processors, spreadsheets and data bases."

Dennis met Beryl Williams at church. Beryl was born at Kingsley Terrace opposite Westgate Hill School. Beryl remembers: "The family moved around the area. We lived at MacDonald Road, Bishop's Road among others – but I grew up at Helen Street. I went to Atkinson Road and South Benwell Schools, then to the College of Commerce at 13. When I left school I worked for Sun Insurance as a shorthand typist. I later worked at Dunston Power Station for a while. There were 500 men and five of us girls, we were spoilt. I was only there from 1959-1961." Dennis recalls: "We were married in 1958 at Paradise Methodist Church on Atkinson Road. The first accommodation for us was on the top floor in the Hydraulic Crane pub on Scotswood Road. The pub was run by Beryl's uncle Jackie Flint and his wife Phemie. It was a free house, Ind Coope and Allsopp Breweries. There were trains on

Atkinson Road Primary School class in 1937. From left to right, back row: ?, Billy Moffatt, ?, ?, ?, Fred Young, ?. 2nd back row. ?,?, Dorothy Barlow, Sybil Scott, ?, Lilian Little, ?, Moira Proud. 3rd row: Patricia Proud, Beryl Williams, George Reed, Audrey Nichol, Eunice Armstrong, ?, Patricia ?. Front row: ? Snowball, ?, Walter Ritson, John Brodie, ?, Violet Carey, ?.

one side and buses on the other. When anything went past the objects in the sideboard rattled together. On the front of the building there were two big attic windows and a smaller one in the middle. The west side was our lounge and next door our bedroom. A long room with a fanlight on the back of the building was converted into a kitchen. We had no view out to the river, but to the front there were four storey houses and we could see right into their rooms. I kept my motorbike in the cellar."

Beryl remembered that Dennis missed the 1962 Blaydon Races celebrations in June. He was in Northern Ireland running a camp for the Newcastle Battalion Boys' Brigade. "My uncle Jackie had a float which went past the pub. There were chairs outside and everyone had a good time. Our first child, Jane was born in July 1962. John was born in 1964 and Helen in 1967. Dennis has been an active member of the Methodist church over the years. He has been a property, church and circuit steward as well as youth leader and Sunday School teacher. He is a lay preacher in the Methodist, and is involved in the training of new lay preachers.

Paradise Methodist Church in 1906.

A Walk up the Pike
by Des Walton

I remember starting to walk up the pike when I was seventeen in 1937. Later I found that Westgate Road and West Road had once been called the West Turnpike Road. So we were still using an old name. The turnpike road to Carlisle had been built in the 18th century partly on the line of the Roman Wall – but it wasn't until the 1820s that a

housing estate called Arthur's Hill was established at the top of Westgate Hill (Later Big Lamp). Isaac Cookson bought the land and named the streets after his sons John, Edward and William and the estate after his other son Arthur. The houses were still there in the 1930s when the whole Arthur's Hill suburb was built up in terraced houses to the Newcastle General Hospital and Union Workhouse.

Below: William Street was named after the son of Isaac Cookson. Notice how narrow the old cobbled back lane is. There were usually archways to allow horses through.

Westgate Road and the West Road which was known by Des and his pals as "The pike". Notice the railings to the graveyard on the right – they curve outwards at the top, this was to discourage burglars raiding graves.

While walking to school in Bath Lane from my home in 73 Brighton Grove near the park in 1935, I remember passing the end of Centre Street which was in a tough area near St James' Park. The whole street was having a party to celebrate the Golden Jubilee of King George V. Such parties were held throughout the country.

Clearance started about 1945 and when I returned home after demob in 1946 I found new prefabs faced Westgate Hill cemetery opposite before the flats were built. To get away from the crowded streets around Westgate Road on a Sunday night the custom grew to promenade up to the west past the fields of Fenham which were not built on until 1900. I joined the walk at the top of Brighton Grove and reached the border of Benwell where the name changed to the West Road.

My main pal, Mervyn Adamson lived at 182 Ellesmere Road near where this part of the West Road was a seething mass of excited walkers. I'd met him there having passed the Brighton and Plaza cinemas – all closed for Sundays. Only Riales ice cream parlour was opened before we reached the Milvain Club (today a Hindu Temple). Beyond, was a large field up to the site of the reservoir – which had been built on the site of Condercum Roman Fort. Later, Rutherford's two schools – both boys and girls moved there after being used as an anti-aircraft base. At the high point there was a gate leading to a path off North – we called the entrance Fat Man Squeeze.

Many people remember the Eldorado Ice Cream carts with the caption "Stop me and buy one". Ice cream blocks were later called ice cream sandwiches – the block in between two wafers.

We'd meet our old school pals such as Scott Dobson, who later wrote and illustrated *Larn Yersel Geordie* and Cliff Heppell. They later met each other in an Indian Army Camp. Cliff's father Jack was solo pianist at the Milvain Club and in the 1920s he also had a band at the Bond Street Baths – off Adelaide Terrace. The baths used to be covered over for dancing for part of the year. Cliff was also a dance band musician later. Mervyn was killed when his naval ship was bombed and sunk in the Mediterranean in 1941 when aged 21. The wartime street blackouts from September 1939 put an end to the "pike" Sunday night promenades enjoyed by so many who often came from miles around to see and be seen. Some would take a circular route down Two Balls Lane, renamed Lonnen – past Fenham Hall and along Bird Cage Walk through Nun's Moor Park – then home to Arthur's Hill.

Cliff Heppell on his bike (left) with children from across the road.

I joined the staff at Fenham Library when it opened in 1938. We were all males and by 1940 we were mostly elsewhere in uniform. I spent six months in what had been Billy Butlin's Holiday Camp in Skegness training to be a telegraphist before taking passage to Liverpool via Cape Town and Mombasa to a cruiser based at Aden. I had my 21st birthday on the way to Aden on the Indian Ocean. Most of the next few years were spent in the tropics visiting ports and countries of the declining British Empire. I even bumped into two people I had last seen "Up the pike" while ashore – one in Cape Town and one in Rangoon, Burma after the defeat of the Japanese.

Before VJ Day Scott Dobson and Cliff Heppell had met while taking part in a concert party in Deolali camp in India which was being produced by Jim Perry. After the war Jim was responsible for writing several TV series including *It Ain't Half Hot Mum*,

Hi-Di-Hi and *Dad's Army*. Scott was helping with the entertainment and painting the sets. In later years Cliff became a piano tuner and up until the time he died he was still tuning my piano. Throughout my whole time in the service of my country – while I was away – all I ever thought of was Newcastle and especially those carefree faces on the "pike".

When I was demobbed in 1946 there was a period when I went back to college for a year. Then I got a job as a librarian at Scotswood Library. I met Councillor Theresa (née Science) Russell who was the wife of the local doctor Harry Russell. She was a strong character and she believed in getting to know the local people. I was encouraged by her to set up a play and reading circle and a music circle at the library. She was the second lady lord mayor in Newcastle and her husband became lord mayor also.

She took me to a dance hall on Scotswood Road which was next door to the Ord Arms near Harold Street. It was an old people's meeting place. Alma Wheeler's family had owned the dance hall which was also used for roller skating.

Being Jewish, Theresa didn't use her ration of bacon. "We sell raffle tickets in aid of the club," she told me, "To see who will win the bacon." Alma worked in the personnel department of Armstrong's factory on

Des in his role in charge of Scotswood Library in the 1950s.

Scotswood Road and when the firm was taken over she arranged for my group to exhibit photos in the works depicting its history. Since then she has been a prominent Scotswood resident on committees planning the future of the area. One of her ancestors was killed in the Montagu Pit Disaster (1925) and both of us have given talks on the subject. My scrap book of press cuttings and articles has now been presented to the community.

I met a lady who was later to become my wife on the staff at Scotswood Library and we got married a few years later. I moved as a librarian to Elswick. I remember that some libraries had a magazine room with newspapers. They found that they had to black out the racing pages as it encouraged bookies to come into the building to take bets. I felt that it was my responsibility to form links with schools. I remember going to a Catholic school when a nun asked me to wait. I discovered that she was very thorough. She rang where I was working and said: "I have someone here declaring to be a librarian!"

I approached Elswick Road School and suggested that it would be useful as they were closing soon to take the children on a tour around nearby sites connected with Sir William Haswell Stephenson who'd lived at Elswick House west of the park. I told them that Richard Grainger had lived in Elswick Hall in the park. I also showed them a fountain in memory of men like Stephenson who'd bought land and presented it to the corporation for the park to be built. Until 1930 the Hall was called the "Model House" as it contained models of the sculptures of John Graham Lough. His George Stephenson monument is on Westgate Road.

When I was based at Elswick Library in the 1950s I believed in getting involved with the local people such as Jimmy Forsyth. Later as area librarian I started to build up a collection of photographs of West Newcastle, including those taken by Jimmy. Phil Kitchen and another community worker wanted to make use of my help when setting up a local history group in Elswick in the Havelock building which was attached to St Paul's Church. We published two booklets – one of them was because several of the people in the group had worked for Richardson's Leatherworks. Phil Kitchen was very keen to get their memories. I collected photographs and had them copied and added to the collection. I was in contact with members of the Richardson family who were still living in the West End. Phil was responsible for the reminiscence work and I was a kind of secretary to help the booklet to be published.

On a fact finding tour of Elswick Park in the 1980s. The house within the park was Elswick Hall once the home of Richard Grainger.

Sir Ralph Richardson, the actor, was a family member and as a boy visited his grandmother living on Elswick Road. By chance he was in a play at the Theatre Royal while we were working on the booklet so we sent him a letter – to which he replied.

With my interest in other religions in West Newcastle, we got together a group of people representing the other sects and a book titled "Newcastle New Era" was published later. We were invited to the Gurdwara near the Big Lamp where the Sikhs met. I went to a service and as a Methodist – I was interested in the customs of the other churches. First of all you went in and sat on the floor where the service was going on. Afterwards we went into another room where we again sat on the floor and were served food. I met a local Methodist lay preacher there called Dennis Carss who had been a resident in the area. He had originally attended the Elswick Road Methodist Church. I was also present when this building was officially handed over to the Muslim Community on Malvern Street.

Nowadays I go to Dilston Road Methodist luncheon club and I'm picked up by an Age Concern bus – I discovered that some of the people live in Benwell. I find myself going around parts of Benwell some of which I have never seen before. One lady in particular who is 95 asked me to contribute to the project of the history of St James' Parish Church to which she attends. My contribution to the history of the churches in West Newcastle is that twenty years ago I wrote two articles for

Richardson's Leatherworks aerial view, 1930.

magazines. In each case I have just had requests for them to be republished. One of them on Sir William Haswell Stephenson who financed the building of three branch libraries including one in Elswick (1890). I was fortunate in meeting a contemporary of mine, John Stephenson – a relation to him who owned the family archives mainly compiled by Sir William's daughter. He allowed me to borrow some, including pre 1920 press cuttings and photographs and deposit them in the collection. My article "The Stephensons of Throckley and Newcastle" traced back to the 18th century when another John Stephenson sold land to John Wesley to build a third Methodist centre in the country. A plaque in Northumberland Street marks the spot – he called it "The Orphan House" even though no orphans actually went there.

The other book is on a man who came from a very well known Methodist family. This year is the centenary of Darras Hall and in the 1890s the organisation was formed called the Northern Allotment Society. They were a group of businessmen – one of them was called Joseph Wakinshaw. He was concerned that nearly all the Arthur's Hill and Elswick area was covered with long rows of terraced houses without gardens. In 1890 the new society leased land from the Corporation and Freemen to form the Nuns Moor Allotment Garden.

Wakinshaw got a group together to buy land on Stamfordham Road – the Red Cow Farm. My grandfather and his building partner had come from Kendal and bought an acre on which to build adjacent homes for their families. They still stand today in the suburb of Westerhope, a name given in 1895 when my mother was a new baby in Kendal Green West. Wakinshaw lived opposite in "Runnymede" and gave the name to the first road in Darras Hall a century ago. The local history society is now reprinting the article.

Phil Kitchen is a guest at Des Walton's 90th birthday party held at Fenham Library. They have lots of memories to share of their time working together on local history. Arthur Frelford and Bill Rosser are to the right.

When I had my 90th birthday party lots of the people who I had become acquainted with were there. It gives me a great lot of pleasure to know that I haven't been forgotten.

After Jimmy Forsyth had left his flat near Scotswood Road I visited him in the care home. I visited him when he was 90 – the age I am now. On another occasion they had invited the press in and I suggested that I could bring some slides along to show his photo and also that it might be a good idea to get hold of a guitarist who had composed The Ballad of Jimmy Forsyth. I have a cd of the music.

In the last year we have seen the death of Jimmy. I discovered when I went to visit him in the Elswick Hall Care Home, that just a few yards away was the building where I was born. Yvonne Young asked me if I could hold a slide show of Jimmy's photos in the new West End Library. She arranged with Sandra Smith the manager and Kelly – activities co-ordinator to bring him to the library. I got a big surprise when I started talking – he was wheeled into the room – Jimmy wanted to join in and we had a kind of a duet. He was 95 and he didn't stay long. Sadly we gathered at the West Road Crematorium a couple of months later for the funeral. The last book about him was on the 1950s and '60s and was published soon after. I am proud to have dedicated a huge part of my life to the subject of Jimmy's life and work.

A Little Bit of Cornish Pasty and a Little Drop of Brown Ale
by Lorna Henwood

Lorna Henwood was born on 1st March 1919. She was christened at St James' Church, Benwell. Her parents were Alice and Thomas and her siblings Leonard, Joyce and Olga. Olga died aged eighteen months during the Spanish Flu epidemic which swept around the world leaving an estimated 50 million dead and 100 million infected. "As a child, from four years of age, I attended the Madam Duke Rose School of Dancing. Florence and Walter Neil took the lessons. I also loved reading."

Lorna was born in 1918. This photo was taken in 1910 when Bramble's shop was doing a roaring trade. Her mother walked along here towards High Cross farm to buy milk.

Lorna could read from an early age. She used to pinch her brother's books and magazines the *Wizard, Hotspur, Billy Bunter* and *Magnet*. "He was five years older than me. I also pinched dad's westerns. I never liked romances so I didn't read *The Red Star* and *Red Letter*. I liked *The Picture Goer* with film stars in. There was a box under the bed full of magazines. I went to see *King Kong* with Faye Wray. She screamed from beginning to end. King Kong held her in his hand like a little broken doll. I was amazed to see how they created him climbing up the building and catching the planes."

Lorna used to walk up Rye Hill, go along Westmorland Road and through Elswick Park on her way to 34 Adelaide Terrace in the summer. It was a penny for a tram car from Rye Hill to Storeys on Clara Street. Even in the winter Lorna went the same route. "The clinic is in the same spot where no 34 used to be. If we had got on at Rye Hill we would have had to pay a penny. So we walked along to Gloucester Street where it only cost us half a penny. There were no trams then over the High Level it was a horse bus over, just as far as the Castle Keep. When they built the Tyne Bridge I was 9 years old. I've still got the book commemorating it from school. Then there were extended lines to Central. Cars only went as far as Central Station."

Rye Hill looking south towards Scotswood Road with People's Hall. Cambridge Street School is to the right.

Spring cleaning was when all of the ornaments came out of the china cabinet. Lorna's dad used to beat the mats in the back lane and whitewash the walls. Venetian blinds in the front room were also cleaned. Those who couldn't afford them used a paper roller blind at the back. She remembers her mam saying "She never whitens her step!" It was noticed if anyone didn't do this.

Lorna wearing her green dress which she wore at her dancing classes.

"Mam used to go along to High Cross farm in Benwell to buy fresh milk. I still remember our Co-op dividend number – 64136. My cousin lived at 42 Atkinson Road. I came over in the school holidays and played with Betty Holmes in Helen Street back lane. My cousin Dora (Dorothy) wanted to go to the pictures on Scotswood Road, we had no money – it was 3d each. Dora went to get an orange box from Buddle Road shops, chopped them to make sticks to sell for the money to get in."

She loved to get her hands on a catalogue, use a pin and play a game, closed her eyes and see which toy she got. "I spent time making stuff with raffia, a long strip of straw and weaved it in and out – teapot stands and suchlike. You had your skipping rope and kept it in your pocket. If you could find an old tin and a few sticks, we picked clay from the field to make a lamp, stick a candle inside and play 'Jack Shine Your Light'."

There was always a bobby walking the beat, it was always the same fellas, we knew them. The police box was on the corner. If you were 18, you had to be in the house for 10 o'clock unless you were going to 2nd house pictures. We had a get together when we left Benwell – after the party, my mam rolled up the carpets and took them to Sheriff Hill, Gateshead."

Before she joined up Lorna could hear the sirens. This was the signal to head for the air raid shelters. "I was in Dalkeith in Scotland training centre and from there to South Wales. I was at Llanethly holding station before being posted to Llangenick on a farm where I met Gerald – my husband to be. I was at Exford all summer and it was love at first sight. He was the first one to speak to me in Exford. I was in a Nissen Hut, they put me on duties to clean it up. He asked "What are you doing here?" and when I answered "Aa divn't naar." He knew that I was from the North East. The hut had a big round corrugated iron stove in the middle of 12-14 beds. It wasn't too bad as in the winter stoves kept the place warm."

They actually had an electric dish washing machine. Lorna thought it was state of the art as it cleaned up plates after 200 men every dinner time, breakfast and tea.

"The middle section was for cold water and on the other side cold clear water. We switched the electricity on, pushed the plate under as the wheels went around, rinsed it off then into the clean water, when it was full we took it onto the bench and put another one in. I used to hate washing up the tins after the cooks. After dinner, washing was the worse time. Some cooks were helpful. Others just chucked them down any old way. Prisoners of war worked in the cook house – Italians, Germans and Russians and we sent them home speaking Geordie, especially the Russians they were canny lads. Some ended up staying on especially those on farm work. We never thought of them as the enemy, we weren't frightened of them."

Posing outside one of the Nissen huts during her time in the regular army – Lorna looks very smart.

Ten days in the Jankers meant being in the cook house peeling spuds. Confined to barracks with hundreds of tatties, spud bashing. Lorna didn't mind if she was late that was her punishment, peeling potatoes. "I was in the regular army for four years – I really enjoyed myself. When I was at Catterick I could get home for the weekend. When I was demobbed, I went back to Pelaw to work. The old routine had all changed, all my friends had gone, I didn't like it. I had worked there at 14 until I joined the army. I used to cycle along Sunderland Road, to church then up to Pelaw. I remembered that when I left school on the Friday and I started work that following Monday for 6 shillings a week. I sometimes caught the tram. If I was late I

Lorna and pals at the book club in the West End Library. Included are: Elsie Dixon, Jean Corbett, John Atkinson from Adult & Culture Service Transport and Lorna Henwood.

used to get a workman's ticket for the two cars – I had to buy two books of tickets."

Lorna was married in September 1947 on a Sunday at a Methodist Church at Salthouse Bank, Low Fell. She came back to live in Benwell. Their marriage lasted for 62 years. Her husband was eight years older than her. "I kept up with the queen over the years. She was married in November 1947. Charles was born the same year as our Kathleen, 1948. Our Gordon and Princess Anne – born in 1950. Then Richard and Geoffrey were born. Elizabeth and I both had four children so I'd been in good company."

Lorna and Gerald Henwood on a day out at the beach.

"My mother's uncle, Matt Alexander was a sign writer and painter. My husband worked for them as a painter. He was 30 when he came here to live at Aunt Nellie's house in Durham Street. When her daughter in law died she went to look after her son and she let us have the house. I also lived at Delaval Gardens, Isabella Close, Burny Close and here at Manisty House. When I go to the chiropodists across the road, I look out at the same view where my aunt Nellie and my cousin Leslie lived."

Lorna at home in Manisty House. Her family collected a selection of photos from her life to create this collage.

"I still kept in touch with some of the girls from the army until recently, they've all gone now. I can still remember my army number – 121119. It's strange to think that I watched the old Sutton's Dwellings being built in the 1930s which stood here before Manisty House. I always say when I walk through to the bedroom "I'm going upstairs." Even though the flat is on the same level. Old habits die hard."

"My Grandmother is buried in St James' churchyard and my grandfather at West Road cemetery. It had just opened it and he was one of the first to be buried there. When we were clearing the house after dad died we found photos of my brother and a whole lot more. My family made a collage with everyone on it and of me and my husband when we were young. I've got two great, great grandsons. I often look back on my happy memories."

"My husband, Gerald was born in Newquay, Cornwall. I will always remember when we went to the beach we used to say – "A little bit of Cornish Pasty and a little bit of Brown Ale go well together.""

There Was Always Music in the House
by Geordie Brannen

George was born in 1943 at 80 Frank Street and his granny Brannen, on his dad's side of the family lived at No 78. He got Geordie from his friends. Geordie's dad worked for Vickers at Water Street.

The Baptist Church hall played a big part in his life. "My mam had worked as a silver service maid when she was younger. In Benwell she was the caretaker at the Baptist Church on Frank Street. She often gave me the keys to the building when it wasn't being used. I rode my sister Betty's bike around the big hall and once hit the rails and went flying over the top. We sometimes played football in the hall. I was a member of the boys' brigade and I played the drums, I was in the middle and Colin Madison and George Salmon were on either side of me. Our group only had three drummers, but Atkinson Road 25th was the posh one with ten – they also had a girls' brigade. We used to march around the streets playing on Good Friday. We started off on spare ground outside the Majestic Cinema, down Atkinson Road to Buddle Road, Elswick Road and back to where we'd started. Everyone split up then and our brigade went back to the Baptists hall where we each got an orange and an apple."

Geordie Brannen with pal Ronnie Hopper. The photo was taken in Frank Street back lane. Notice Geordie's jazzy jumper.

"I paid Mrs Wilkinson one and sixpence a lesson, she lived at Gerald Street. If I hadn't been practising, I gave it a miss and carried on to the Grand Cinema and take my music case with me. I learned how to play the piano and I had a fiddle. I took it to school one day and Mr Heads, a master asked if I would sell it. I got £10 for it."

Geordie laughed as he remembered one occasion when local lad Jimmy Lucas had toothache. "We were upstairs where all the weights were kept under the stage. Jimmy had toothache and someone suggested that he pull the tooth out. He just picked up a pair of pliers and yanked it out. It wouldn't stop bleeding and he had to go to hospital. Jimmy worked on the rings and the bars, he was a strong bloke. Once, he was lying down on the floor lifting the weights, everyone egged him on to lift, just one more, just one more, go on, another. He dropped the weights down onto his chest and he was still ok. It weighed 300 lbs. He was known as the Genie because of his bald head. I enjoyed weight lifting and I also went to Grainger Park club where I was once knocked out." When Geordie left he joined the 8th Tyne Valley

Geordie's mother Ginny in her position as a silver service maid.

The Grainger Park Boys' Club on Scotswood Road had previously been the Vulcan pub. The club later moved to Armstrong Road.

Brigade at Lemington. The meetings were held in Jim's Hut. He learned to play the bugle.

Geordie remembers the deep snow of 1958. "When we opened the front door the snow was solid up in front of us. We dug a three feet channel through the snow from our house to Elsie Clabbie's shop. We dug through to Mrs Davison's house and to Mrs Miller's across the road. In the winter my mam always got the tin bath off the nail on the wall and put it near the fire for our bath. Our clothes were always put on the fender to warm up. I used to chuck the water down the back stone steps, but one night when I threw it down, I didn't see dad and he got the whole lot, he was soaking wet. He also came a cropper on another occasion when he went to the toilet. We used to keep a jam jar with paraffin inside and a piece of pyjama cord as a wick. It kept the pipes warm in winter. His shirt tail caught fire as he stood up. He was jumping around all over the place to put it out."

During the summer weeks Geordie helped out at Elsie Clabbie's shop. "I was about twelve years old. The shop had wooden shutters with slats at the bottom where they fixed on. In the morning I took them off. She used to give me a bag full of sweets in payment, but I don't know how she made any profit, there were Crunchies, bars of chocolate and lots of those little sugar dummies. I used to come home with empty boxes. Mrs Simons took over the business after Elsie left."

Geordie attended South Benwell School. Arthur Brayson, Ken Brown and Mick Graham were in his class. He lived on Greenhow Place where the cobblers stood at the top of the street.

One character who George remembers also lived in Frank Street. "Old Albert, I remember how he always came to the front door wearing his medals. He wore one of those German style macs, khaki coloured and really long, just like the ones that you see on *Allo Allo*. The house was used to film *Get Carter*. All the neighbours were gossiping, saying that the film crew had spent thousands on doing the place up. They had only decorated and put new lino down. The funeral car came down the lane and they brought a coffin out, it continued on down to Scotswood Road. When filming had finished, someone broke in and stole the lino."

A neighbour, Cyril kept hens, they used to walk the top of the walls in Maughan Street. "There was always music in the house. Dad played the drums in a group called The Merrymakers. They played at the Old Hall Social Club. He also toured around the Co-op halls such as Loadman Street, Buckingham Street, Scotswood Road and in the pubs in the area such as the Delaval Arms. I don't know how he

The back yard of the Hydraulic Crane. Everyone is dressed up to celebrate the Coronation of George VI in 1937.

managed to get around up those steep streets, he only had one leg. Even in the winter he'd be struggling with the drum under one arm. He sometimes used a crutch and other times his false leg. When dad left the band he sold the drums to local shop owner, Reggie Moore who gave them to his son Peter. I remember that Reggie used to make forts and castles from wood."

Pigeons were another interest for the Brannen family. "Stan Chisholm worked at a butchers shop on the West Road, he used to sing in the clubs and he also kept pigeons. Jacky Coulson was the pigeon lad. Stan gave me two pigeons and I had nowhere to keep them so I put them in the toilet cistern. Dad was on constant night shift. He was on his way to the house and he went to the toilet. He got the shock of his life when he heard the coo cooing behind him. Kenny Brown's dad kept pigeons in the Tan Yards. He had bus seats on the gantry – two double seats with ash trays on them – he'd sit there shaking the tin with seeds in. We had to sit really still until the birds were back in. The road went down by Mitchell Bearings so we were looking down towards the railway line. Mr Brown took the rings off their legs then clocked them in."

A trip from the Old Hall Social Club which was on Edward Gardens. The men took musical instruments with them for the entertainment. George Brannen snr is playing the mouthorgan on his "One man band" with a tambourine on the top.

Geordie remembers when he got his first car. He used to look at the vehicles at Moore's Motors on the West Road just past the General Hospital. "It was a lovely pea green mini. I took dad up to see it and he said "It's not finished, the bonnet hasn't been painted!" I told him that it was a rally car. It had a big gear stick and a little one at the side. Mr Moore recognised us because the family had bought his wife's car. Dad said to me "Right son, you get inside the car, I'm having a word with Mr Moore." The next thing I heard was "Your car will be washed, polished and ready in a couple of days."

Geordie was surprised that his dad put up the money because he had put up the cash before for a motorbike. He'd paid £207 for Geordie to own an excelsior 197. It was delivered to the door complete with safety helmet and goggles. "I never passed my test for the bike – it was delivered to the door. Stan Corkhill gave me a hand to take it off the stand. I got on and we went along Grainger Park Road, Stan on the back and me on the front. I took it up Lemington, onto the West Road past the orphanage, I went one way and the bike went the other. I remember mam taking the bits of gravel out of my back and putting Dettol on. Some blokes came down our lane carrying out repairs on the walls, one of them asked if it was my bike and if I wanted to sell it. I gave it to him for £25. When dad came back home after his shift, he asked where the bike was. When he found out how much I had let it go for, the crutch came out from under his arm. He couldn't believe it, the bike only had 1,000 miles on the clock. I got a hiding."

His auntie Mary Burkett called at the Brannen home with a radio as a present for Geordie's car. "We had to sit in the front seat to hear it and when I went

Geordie Brannen at his sister's marriage to Don Atkin. This was an extra special day for Geordie as he was wearing his first pair of long trousers.

around corners, I had to hold onto it because the lid fell down. It was so heavy that I was always knackered when I got where I was going. It wasn't an ideal set up so I took it into the house. Whenever aunt Mary came to the house, everyone shouted "Quick, here's aunt Mary, get the radio out!" I've still got it, it's in the loft. The next thing she gave me was a nodding dog. Another thing that I've still kept all these years later is my boys' brigade cap."

Geordie married Maureen in 1967 at Sugley Church in Bell's Close Lemington. They have children Jason, born in 1970, and Michaela born in 1974. The couple live in Westerhope where Geordie still has many hobbies. He has built his own aviary where he kept cockatiels, Bengalese, goudians and Zebra finches. Maureen says "My family thought the world of Geordie, he couldn't do any wrong. He was spoilt in both houses."

Geordie pictured outside Maureen's house on Union Hall Road, Lemington. The car was pea green and he can still remember the registration number – 768 6UP.

48

I Was a Sunbeam
by Betty Atkin

Betty was born on Armstrong Road and soon after she lived at Rendle Street in Elswick. Her mam then got a house at number 80 Frank Street. "I don't remember much from Rendle Street as I was very young when we left there, but I do recall Mrs Gilmore who lived there, she used to be a barmaid. My granny lived downstairs at 78 Frank Street and the Barclays and Mary Park lived at 82. I remember Peter Connelly lived on Buddle Road in the back lane part near the gardens, there were three or four families to a yard. Peter is my daughter-in-law's dad."

Other folks that Betty remembers from the area. "Elsie Robson lived in Greenhow Place near Edgeware Road, she used to take me to the dance at Loadman Street Hall. My dad used to sometimes play there for weddings and parties. My aunt Olive and uncle Willie lived in Loadman Street near the McDougalls. Stan Chisholm also lived in Frank Street, he had a butcher's shop on the West Road at the top of Ellesmere, there was a Post Office at the opposite corner. Stan kept pigeons, he once gave our George a couple and he hid them in the toilet cistern."

Betty standing in school yard with pals. She is pictured fourth from the left.

Betty was evacuated during the war years to Alston. "My mam came with me. We stayed at the Sun Hostel which was up the bank in a kind of shed – pagoda style. We were all sent to the local church to be picked. All of the Davison family from Frank Street were put in the hostel too. Mam could only stay with me there for a month and she had to go back, so I was left on my own. One by one we all got billeted to live in someone's home from the village. I went with Mrs Jackson, she lived right at the top of the bank in a little cottage – I remember she had a little wall covered in nasturtiums. The first time I went back there years later, there was still the cobbled street, the market square on a slope. Back home my nana was an auxiliary nurse. Both nana and granddad were British Legioners, they did a lot of fundraising and selling poppies."

Betty attended South Benwell School. "I was there until I was about 13 or 14 and then I went up to Atkinson Road Secondary. At the side of the building was a house-craft flat. One week we were taught cookery and the next, laundry. We put the flat iron on a bracket to heat up, but at home we put it on the gas heating. When ironing a

Betty singing on stage with the Merrymakers Band. Her father George Brannen snr is playing drums.

shirt, we were told to start with the back and top, then collar, body then sleeves. I liked needlework. Mrs Bell was my form teacher. The lads did woodwork or metalwork."

Betty enjoyed activities at the Salvation Army Hut. "I was a sunbeam. They used to hold young people's meetings. I was in a few clubs, then the girls' life brigade and youth club – they were held in the church hall of the Baptists' Church on Frank Street. My mam and dad cleaned the building, we lived across the road. We went on trips from Sunday school on the train. We boarded at Elswick Station and went to Ryton Willis for a picnic. I can still see the mothers hanging out of the windows, they pulled up the sash windows shouting "Tara, have a good time." I also enjoyed going to the Old Hall Social Club trips, my dad played in the Merrymakers at the club. I sometimes sang on the stage with the band."

Betty worked in the tank shop at Vickers as a pin driller. "My dad was a store keeper in the tank shop. I met Don Atkin, who was to be my husband at the Elswick end of the works beside the toll bar, the Water Street side. Don was working on a lathe. Don was born in Brewery Street. The family moved to Bath Lane Terrace. He used to go to St Mary's School then on to St Aloysius. He remembered the VE (Victory in Europe) party which was held on Bath Lane Terrace, we have a photo of the day, every one is having a good time."

Don Atkin on the left waits for his drink to be served on VE day in 1945. The photo was taken in Bath Lane.

"Aa'm From Newcastle Man!"
by Younes Mohammed

Younes was born in 1954 in Kashmir, Pakistan. He was five years old when he came to live in Newcastle. His dad worked for British Engines in Byker which involved casting and putting hot metal into moulds. Younes attended Cambridge Street School in Elswick. Teachers he remembers were head teacher Miss Brown and his form teacher Miss Hannah. "All of the lessons were held in the same room, our own form room. There was a teacher called Mr Penman, he had a very stern look, a disciplinarian. He had the effect of making you shiver, even if you hadn't done anything. A bit like when we saw a policeman and we hid behind a car and we were totally innocent. I enjoyed watching Newcastle United matches. The first match I saw was a Fairs Cup game against a Hungarian Team."

Younes lived at 37 Hawthorne Street in Cruddas Park. "When we came in the front door, it was split into two flats, we lived in the upper flat. The living room area looked onto the front street. There were two bedrooms, one at the back and one at the front with a big extension with bathroom and toilet. There was no central heating, but it was quite rare to have a toilet inside in those days and we also had a hot water heater."

Younes attended Cambridge Street School. This photo was taken in 1964.

He enjoyed playing outdoors in Elswick. "The majority of the houses around us were derelict, we used to play in them. We went into the Elswick Park to play cricket and to ride on our bogeys which we had made ourselves from wooden crates from a shop. The park was so near that in the summer it was a continuous trek from home to the park and back. I took my bike up there when I was seven years old. In winter we went down the steep cobbled streets on our sledges. I remember the winter of 1961. We were blocked in by the heavy fall of snow. People had dug trenches and it was so high I couldn't see over the top."

Younes attends the mosque on Malvern Street, The Bilal. "The first mosque that I remember was in an old Victorian house which stood about three or four along from St Michael's church on Westmorland Road. It was a place for people to meet and socialise. It was the first mosque in Newcastle. There was also a mosque in East Parade next to Rye Hill."

Cooking was a central focus of life at his home. "My mam enjoyed cooking and I used to help her to peel the vegetables. I used to prepare karela, a kind of bitter lemon. We fried them and stuffed them with mince. I helped to stir the onions. It was all good practice – I could see everything that was being made and I picked it up. Puddings were usually Indian sweets like lado or coconut and my favourite was jalebi."

I took this photo in 2010 at Malvern Street Mosque. I was welcomed into the calm and peaceful atmosphere of the building. From left to right: Zafar Iqbal, Qari Saeed, Mr Taj Malik, Haji Hakeem and Wazir Ahmed.

An awesome sight – the chandelier inside the dome of the Malvern Street Mosque.

When Hawthorn Street was demolished the family moved to Ashfield Terrace West. Younes attended Slatyford School. "Teachers I remember from that school were Mr Hackett, Mr Thornton, my house teacher Mr Trotter, form teacher Mr Brennan. My favourite lesson was science. I was about to be made prefect when I was in the 4th or 5th form. Me and a few of my mates were acting on in the corridor and someone fell over and was hurt, not seriously, but we were called in to the office. I wasn't the culprit but I was warned that if I was to be prefect I should behave in a way that others could look up to. I did get the job."

Younes went on holiday to Pakistan with his father when he was about fourteen years old. "I came back on the plane earlier than dad because I had to get back to school for the new term. As my passport was from when I was ten years old, I must have looked a lot different as I was really much broader and taller and I had begun to grow a beard and moustache. The guy at immigration looked at me, then to the photo. He pointed me towards the interview room and asked me in pigeon English "Where … did … you … live … before … you … went … on … holiday?"

"I replied "Newcastle man," In my Geordie accent. He burst out laughing. It turned out that he was from South Shields. He was totally taken aback and laughed "You can fake a passport, but not the accent."

Younes says that in order to 'get' regional jokes you have to understand the slang. "In Pakistan, a rolling pin is called a balentine but pronounced valentine. We joke that over here a card we send in February is a valentine. We send these to appease the wives."

His first job was at Winthrop Laboratories Laboratory. "I had a car by then, I passed my test after the second try. I was a junior scientific officer, I carried out research and development tests. It was routine work which determined whether a product which we were developing was correct. I was there for two and a half years before I left to work for Proctor and Gamble at Longbenton, the work was similar. I tried my hand at my own business and bought a shop at Wrekenton, it was a general dealers. I bought a post office on Armstrong Road next to the Bobby Shafto. Next I went to Pakistan for a holiday, I was away for about a year and when I came back I went onto the taxis. It wasn't difficult learning the streets because I had been brought up in the West End so the routes weren't a problem. I was based in Fenham for Fenham Taxis. I remember once being called out to a wedding. I had the pleasure of collecting the bride, groom and mother and other family members. They were checking with each other, have you got this, that and the other, especially the prospective mother in law. She was ensuring that everyone was sorted out. We got half a mile down the street when she cried out "I've forgotten my teeth!" We had to go back to collect them."

Younes is married with children. His wife is Rashida. Their eldest son is Tariq, next are Yousef, Ilyas, Farzanah (daughter) and Raza. Some of the children attended Todd's Nook Playgroup. It's at this point that I remember working there for a few years and we speak about Jennifer who ran the group with Janet Speight. "I remember that Jennifer used to pick our kids up in her own car to take them to the playgroup."

Younes now runs the Adelaide Post Office on Adelaide Terrace. The shop also has a general dealers in the other half of the shop and his eldest son Tariq helps out there.

Younes behind the counter of his shop/post office on Adelaide Terrace.

All That Jazz
by Keith Crombie

Keith was born in Seaham in 1939. His father was born in Sunderland and was in the merchant navy. Keith still keeps all of his father's discharge papers from his time as a merchant sailor. "When he left they stamped the book. My dad later became a policeman in 1933 and I still have the memorabilia from his time there also. He worked at the West End and was also a station sergeant at Pilgrim Street for a while. My dad's mother came from Sunderland. I have two sisters, Susan who now lives near Blackpool and Janet who lives at Denton Burn."

Canning Street School was where Keith studied. He began school in January 1945. It was during the war years and he remembered seeing the air raid shelters on Colston Street. "The day I started school, there was a big red sun in the sky, we had double summertime. The clocks were put two hours forward to save daylight. One of the masters knew when children had ripped a page out of their books to make a paper aeroplane. We got the belt when he discovered the missing pages. The belts were made from the strips of leather which were used for pulling the train windows open. But there were happy times. On the last day at Christmas we took cakes in for the party, we made lanterns and paper decorations."

Keith with a Henry Moore sculpture.

Keith enjoyed trying to remember all of his classmates. Some of them went on to become well known in the community and also on television. "Pauline Fetter had long ringlets and Edna Tyro lived at the bottom of Tiverton Avenue. Alan Joicey – he lived next door to me in Weidner Road. I sat next to Alan Conway (Cohen) in class. He became the editor of a newspaper in Tel Aviv, he lived in either Ellesmere or Hampstead Road. Others I recall are Marjorie Connor, she had a second hand shop on Elswick Road. Thelma Potts, lived on Hampstead Road, she was dead skinny and eventually became a model. Val McLain acted in comedy on TV – she's Jimmy Nail's sister. Alan Ashman's mam had a shop running parallel to Condercum Road. Ann Lambert went to America, when she came back she worked for a woman who owned a place on the Quayside, the woman left it to her. It had been called Samina Warehouse beside the Guildhall. It later became the Sea Nightclub. I went to a gala once and met her, at first I thought that I was talking to my old teacher until I clicked that it was Ann."

Keith's sisters enjoyed dancing and were members of the Stella Murray School of Dancing. "I used to get dragged into it. Miss Murray had a deaf aid, it was the size of a box Brownie camera, she used to carry it around with her. She was a bit old fashioned. I preferred to be at the St James' church hall in the scouts group. I think it was the 56th division. My dad used to take me to the Carnegie Library on Atkinson Road. Miss Lucie Green was the librarian back then, you didn't dare breathe."

When Keith was a boy, he enjoyed reading books about aeroplanes and ships or Just William and Bertie Wooster. He could read until late at night during the summer months. He also had comics delivered to his home. "I used to get the *Dandy* and our Susan had the *Beano* – Lord Snooty, Desperate Dan, Little Plum, Korky the Kat, Keyhole Kate and Julius Sneezer the Roman Geezer, Black Bob the dog. The comic strips had proper stories. We played hopscotch and Battle of Britain games. We stood cigarette cards up against the wall and pitched at them, if you hit them you claimed them as your own. There was a kite maker in our street, he made them out of brown paper, bits of bamboo cane and glue – he made the tail out of rolled up newspapers.

There were conkers in October, bonfires and roast tatties in November and slides on the ice in December in the school yard."

Jack Batey was a neighbour of Keith's. He owned a garden shed and if anyone wanted something fixed they called on him at 25 Weidner Road. "We lived at number 27. You just had to mention it and he sorted it out. Varnishing, painting, joinery and cobbling, among many other things. His wife Evelyn was a nurse, she was a good woman. Their son Alan served in the Navy during the war on mine sweepers. Eric Armstrong and Bob Trotter used to look after me when I was a kid, they were older than me – we went to Mallaby's to buy Dinkie cars. Bob became a policeman."

Keith wore boots and a mac during the severe winters. He wore a hat, a sou'wester which was in a fisherman's style. "I looked just like the man in the Skippers sardines advert. My great uncle Jack Mennel worked as an artist and he drew the cartoon for that advert. He went to Sunderland Art College. My old man wasn't keen on fashion – he didn't approve of the styles. I used to get my jeans taken in at a house on Croydon Road. I once got a pair of black jeans from London, dad wasn't impressed."

Keith passed for Rutherford School and on leaving he tried his hand at running a second hand shop. He repaired and sold second hand cars for a while at Minories and Blandford Street. Keith also had a garage at Byker. But, Jazz was his main interest. He first took an interest in this music when he lived in Benwell. "I started listening to Jazz when I was about seventeen, with a friend, Jackie Miller. He lived on Condercum Road. On Tuesdays, when his dad went to pay his union dues, we'd put the records on. His dad was a real fan of Acker Bilk, Duke Ellington and Benny Goodman. Jackie worked at Walker's Newsagents shop on the West Road and after he left school he continued to run it. Jackie's sister went out with Hank Rankin, who later became Hank Marvin. He used to live in Stannington Street with his grandma, he also went to Rutherford School. Then I began putting the records on in a church hall in Benwell village next to Wright's sweet shop on the main road.

I was about seventeen when I began putting the records on as well as looking after the Jazz club at Rutherford College. I did work at Parsons for a while, but I was more interested in Jazz. I used to go to the dance at the Venerable Bede church hall with my pal Norman Lines."

Keith met a man called Mike Jeffries who ran the Jazz club in Nelson Street. "Evelyn Patterson had a dance school there and we played Jazz. At the time it was frequented mainly by students. I helped Mike, then he opened the Marimba Coffee Bar on High Bridge Street in the basement near the fire station – it was really adventurous at the

Jess Johnson dressed as Charlie Chaplin and me outside the Jazz Café during a break from a burlesque show by Pink Lane.

time. We liked the classic swing bands and Arty Shaw, Fats Waller. Mike then opened the Downbeat and I spent two years managing the place. He used to enjoy travelling and he went all over the place. I paid the bills for six weeks once when he was away. The license was transferred from there to the Club A Go Go. Then, the blues came in. Eric Burdon and Alan Price from the Animals were there – they all went down to London."

Keith still manages the Jazz Club in Pink Lane where a wide variety of acts can be seen. Among those Pink Lane Poetry and Performance who entertain every second Thursday in the month. He keeps a wide collection of films and books at the cafe and is always visiting art galleries and cinemas. His interested are wide and varied and he packs as much as he can into every day. His philosophy of life is: "The room where you live is just a room."

A Local Lad
by Maurice Morgan

Maurice Morgan was born in 1928 at Providence Terrace in Scotswood. "It was at the bottom of Denton Road before you hit Scotswood Road, right opposite us was Dr Butterfield – he got Cushy as a nickname."

His grandparents on his mother's side were Matthew and Jane (née Brown) Henderson. Her father was a Methodist preacher. Grandfather Henderson was a wherryman and a trade union boss. He pulled the flat barges behind the tugs on the Tyne at Scotswood. "He used to visit the ships as far as the Swing Bridge to Andersons on Bridge Crescent. They used to load fruit onto the boats. Anderson's sold fruit to my granddad."

Maurice married Shirley Sanderson from Shafto Street in 1950 and they have two children – John, born 1952 and Jane 1953. Shirley had trained and worked as a teacher, but settled on a career as a librarian, working in branches at central, Fenham, Scotswood and Benwell Library. Maurice used to wait for her to finish her shift and they would go to the Milvain dance studio or if they had a half day free on Wednesdays to the Oxford tea dances. He was working for R.J. Morpeth carpet furnishers at the time, opposite Eldon Square in Blackett Street. "There also used to be a dance hall where the Bowling Alley is now on the West Road called the Brighton. I used to wear my army suit or my grey flannels and she went in for the new look, flared trousers."

Maurice remembers that show people came to the area once a year and they set up opposite the Majestic Cinema where there was a quarry and allotments. "They came with two shuggy boats and a roundabout and they set up right next to the quarry. One day we were all in the cinema and a lad came rushing in to tell us that there was a dead monkey in the quarry, all the kids ran out to take a look."

He spoke of the folks and trades people in Benwell. Donald Race had a fruit shop half way along on Adelaide Terrace. The grapes were delivered in a huge wooden barrel. Maurice used to work there – he got 6d a week. One of his jobs was to separate

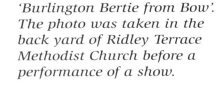

Maurice dressed as 'Burlington Bertie from Bow'. The photo was taken in the back yard of Ridley Terrace Methodist Church before a performance of a show.

the grapes into quarter and half pounds. "There were some characters – one fella – a little pitman who worked in either the Montagu Pit or the Blaydon railway sheds used to like his drink, mainly at the Skiff pub in Blaydon. The Derwenthaugh Staithes were across Scotswood Road, he sometimes went over to the other

Another Skiff pub stood on Scotswood Road and the corner of Dunn Street and Railway Street. This photo was taken in 1956.

side on a Saturday for a drink. One Saturday, he didn't come home. Everyone began searching for him, afraid that he would be found lying out in the cold. Ships came in from Holland to the Staithes to pick up coal and they found his jacket and waistcoat nearby. The river police searched up and down and all along the Tyne up to Ryton and found nothing. A memorial service was held at the church on Whitfield Road. Then it was discovered that he'd been in a fight with the men from the ship, they had knocked him out and put him aboard the boat to Amsterdam. He had to wait for the next colliery boat to bring him back. I remember there used to be a fella who had an allotment on Chapel Bank, near the Sporting Arms. It stood right at the bottom just before you got to Adamsez. He used to talk, talk and talk to you, then he'd say "Divn't keep is taalkin' here aal day man – I want to water the garden before it rains!"

Part of Maurice's business is now in the old Lloyds Bank building. When it was a bank it was only open between ten and twelve each day. "It's in the Kelly's directory – tradespeople had to pay two shillings and sixpence to have an entry in this book. There used to be Mrs Burnett's shop selling ladies' hats nearby. Jimmy her grandson was a pal of mine and we used to go to the matinees together on a Saturday mornings to watch Laurel and Hardy. I remember Shirley Sanderson ran a drama group and they used to practise at the library in Elswick, but there were no changing rooms, so people had to go onto the fire escape to get changed. I remember playing the part of Burlington Bertie from Bow. The plays were performed all over the North. Grenville Banks – whose father had been a minister at Scotswood – taught drama. They were mainly religious plays."

Maurice has preserved many of the original features in the old building – Bakerlite door handles, light switches, fireplaces and he still keeps the old neon ice cream and milk shakes sign which was left from when that part of the building was an ice cream parlour. His desk was bought from Arnott's oil suppliers who were based at Newcastle. "I paid £3 for both desks."

Maurice used to be a youth club leader at Scotswood Methodist Church hall on Ridley Terrace. "Alan Hull, of Lindisfarne, lived in Sutton's Dwellings. They were stuck

Ridley Terrace. The Methodist Church can be seen jutting out on the right side in the distance – a Primitive Methodist church which amalgamated with Whitfield Road Church. Later, the Ridley Terrace building became a youth club where Maurice worked as a youth leader.

for somewhere to practice, so they came for a look around, it was a lovely old building. But on one occasion Lindisfarne were in the hall, they were interviewing a new pianist. There was a grand piano upstairs and they asked to have a try. Later on, after they had left, on the Saturday night the Felling Male Voice Choir came to hold a concert in the chapel. The minister opened the meeting with a prayer and the pianist was a lady wearing a long evening gown. The music was *Guide Me Over Great Jehovah*. But one of the band members had put drawing pins into the hammers, I'd never heard that hymn played quite like that in a honky tonk fashion. I nearly got the sack for that incident. My nephew, Terry Morgan was also in a band, he played guitar."

Maurice keeps track of his business dealings by filing invoices and information on bulldog clips behind his desk. In order, from left to right: the first clip is for clubs, a record of people paying weekly; next are measurements; then estimates; to order; on order; fitting; to charge; people who want a few jobs done, but only one at a time; and finally jobs which are pending. He doesn't need a computer – Maurice knows each and every order which are all kept very methodically.

Maurice called into Craven's regularly on Ridley Terrace. Notice the metal advert signs outside. The front room was made into a shop. Margaret and Johna ran it – his brother Bill managed the Sporting Arms.

Maurice has a fail-safe system of recording orders which are kept on bulldog clips behind his desk.

A Time of Coke Braziers and Blow Lamps
by Ted Clark

Ted was born in 1940 in Longframlington and christened Errol Terence Clark. His great grandfather John Clark had moved from the Elsdon area of north west Northumberland to Elswick. At first, John lodged with his aunt and uncle James Aiken at 11 Worley Street in the 1860s, he worked as a railway wagon driver. He later took an interest in bar work taking employment in several city centre pubs once he got married. Eventually John became owner of some pubs in Sunderland including: the Beehive, the Derby and the Wheatsheaf.

Ted recalls: "I married Maureen Clough who was from Alnwick. In 1962 we lived in a bedsitter at 24 Beechgrove Road. The landlord was Polish. He'd been a pitman, had an accident and set up renting out bedsitters. We were on the middle floor for £2 per week. All of the rooms were taken by other residents." Ted and Maureen have three children John Richard, born 1965, Judith 1967 and Kevin 1972 and five grandchildren.

Ted worked for Newcastle Corporation as a bus conductor in 1962. He remembers "The service No. 9 Blakelaw to Beacon Lough had an open platform at the rear of the bus. The last bus from Blakelaw at the weekend was a problem. The punters would pile on at the Ord Arms at Cowgate – even when the bus was full – at times shuving me into the luggage compartment. One night, the driver had difficulty pulling away. He was in the cab at the front isolated from the passengers. At the terminus, he asked me how many punters were on. I answered "A lot." There were nineteen standing upstairs."

Ted also worked at NEEB in Durham Street. "Before it was nationalised in 1947 during the war it had been known as DISCO. There were two separate companies, privately owned prior to nationalisation. When I was there, a pension scheme was in place, men got discount on electricity, but after nationalisation all concessions went."

Ted was a cable jointer's mate in the west end. He recalled that the starting wage was eight pounds and five shillings per week in 1962. "A craftsman got £12 per week – that was for a fully time served electrician or fitter. I remember Jimmy Forsyth used to take photos of us disconnecting electricity supplies to old

Ted and Maureen Clark on their wedding day in 1962.

properties in the 1960s. We moved around Buddle Road, past Durham Street, Meldon Street, Park Road, Rye Hill, De Grey Street and as far as Cowgate. Jimmy followed us and said "If you want a copy it'll cost you sixpence." We had to use black paint on the house doors to let the demolition squads know that the supply had been disconnected. We used it on lead tubing to seal the end of the cables."

At the time when Ted was working when they started a job, it had to be completed all in the same day. "When we worked it was the time of coke braziers and blow lamps. We had to heat up materials, solders and bitumens to carry out work on cables. In 1963 the adverts for workers were put into the local paper. The dole would send up to ten men along for interviews. The cable jointers all had nicknames such as Yogi

Bear, Bob the blob, Hissing Sid (The foreman), Flash Gordon, One Blonk. I became a shop steward and I was known as Ted the Red."

Ted's family moved to Denton Burn, but he is still involved in local community projects in Benwell. He has been part of the team who have tidied up St James' Church graveyard, a very physical and demanding job of work. Ted attends the monthly slide shows and talks at West End Library and is a member and volunteer for Northumberland and Durham Family History Society.

Above: St James' Church on Benwell Lane. Ted Clark can often be seen caring for the plants and keeping the weeds under control in the grounds. I took this photo from the attic window of Morgan's Carpets at the bottom of Condercum Road.

Left: Ted and Fred Millican pour over local maps at West End Library.

To Australia and Back
by John Hunter

John Hunter was born in Tyne Dock, South Shields. He moved to 87 Amelia Street when he was three years old after his dad was killed in a pit accident. His dad was born at Boldon Colliery and his mother, Elizabeth (née Taylor) was born in Newcastle, she organised charabanc trips to the beach. The local shopkeepers knew her well and they gave her fruit, bakeries gave her two or three days old scones. Everyone had a free apple, orange, cake and a cup of tea. "She was also a social worker in the area, she supported the neighbours when they needed help and she laid out their dead. I used to run the messages. I remember mam was about to lay a woman out. She held the feet, the deceased's husband got the head and we lifted her up onto the table. He didn't know that when a body is moved it sometimes gives out a groan. He got the shock of his life, dropped the body and ran out of the house. Mam explained to him that it was just wind."

When John was older, he and his step dad made proggy and clippy mats. They also made decorations and streamers to sell at Christmas time. People knew what was on offer and they called around to John's home. "I remember one house we lived in on Scotswood Road, there was a little path, it was just feet away from the railway line. When the trains went past, the house shook. There was no electricity, only gas mantles. There were cobble stones on the floor and when we turned the gas mantle off, the cockroaches came out, we could hear them clicking. Then we jumped out with a slipper, it was great fun for us kids."

John Hunter on the left with his mam and dad at the Gun which was run by the boxer Seaman Tommy Watson. The photo was taken in the 1950s on John's return from Australia where he had worked in the gold mines.

John attended St Michael's and St Aloysius schools coming home at lunch times for bread and jam. He grimaced as he recalled the dicky nurse "She used to scrape my head until it was red raw." He left school at the age of twelve because his step father and brother went away to war. "They both went to sort Hitler out, my brother to the Air Force and dad into the Navy. Dad was captured by the Germans, in a way he was far luckier than most. He couldn't swim and was aboard a ship which was taking troops to North America. The ship was attacked and there was burning oil all around. Most of the people who jumped were killed and dad was scared to take the plunge. Four were saved and they became prisoners of war. All of the teachers and most children were evacuated, the schools were closed in our area but I stayed at home because my mam would have been alone. She worked for the railways during the war years. It wasn't until 1947 that I joined up. It was during the worst winter I'd ever known. It snowed from November through until March. I went to Carlisle in the army. When I picked my kit up, I was given a pair of shorts and sandshoes, then sent on a five mile run. Many of us were ready to drop and some did collapse, but not me. I would rather have been fighting the Germans!"

John recalls the war years in Benwell. When the war was on the Germans dropped incendiary bombs. "They thought that they were going to win the war if they hit Vickers – they came pretty near. There were lots of areas with houses missing around Benwell. A fire bomb fell down our chimney, luckily it stuck halfway down, we stood outside looking up and watching as it flared. It was like snow coming down. I went to St Michael's later in the morning and bombs had fallen down behind the alter. It had pumped in so much water – I had to plodge into the church."

John has worked for many companies and had a variety of careers. "I was working at the council on pest control, everyone said "There's the rat catcher." I was recognised wherever I went because most people had need of the service. The Co-op paid the council once a month to check for rats and mice. I got to know all of the staff, it was like one big family. I also worked in the Adamsez building checking for rats and mice. We worked with a sense of humour – we'd often see women running screaming up the lanes. There were eight of us on the team, we were all good friends. We got to know all of the customers and bosses at the companies."

If there was a football match on Wednesdays John and his mates all got the best seats free of charge. They had front seats at the cinema on Mondays and sometimes saw films screened before the general public. It was the same at the fairground, free rides. "They really looked after us. Whenever we told anyone what our job was, they always said that they could never do the job, but we loved it. No one bothered us, we went to a job and they just said "Right, go on, they're in there." Then they went away. The traps or poison was laid and left to do the work. It was like a polis in a park job. There were lots of rats at the Quayside. The worse place to work was at the cattle market. There was so much blood running among the cobbles, it attracted them. They were getting the best food. Rats sometimes ran up my trouser leg. I used to see the herdsmen coming along the road using a stick to hurry the cattle along." John jokes "At least the bulls didn't run up my trouser leg."

John tried his hand at gold mining in Australia, he emigrated there in the 1940s. He stayed for five years and learned how to converse in many languages. When John came back to Newcastle, he registered with a Polish doctor. "It was in the 1950s. I said "Good morning and how are you" in his language and he was really surprised. I had learned a little of various languages that I had picked up from the men I worked with. We remain good friends to this day. He was known as Dr Adams to locals because most people couldn't pronounce his name."

"I went to the Ord Arms in Scotswood when I first came back and saw this girl, her name was Ann Paxton and she had just been demobbed from the Air Force. We just clicked straight away and have been together ever since. She was born in Scotswood and lived in Yewcroft Avenue and worked at Custombilt washing cars."

John and Ann were married at Newcastle Civic Centre and he jokes "We've been together fifty one years and I've still got the scars."

Seaman Tommy Watson

The Ord Arms where John first took a shine to Ann Paxton. The clock on top of the pub was later transferred to a brewery building when the pub was demolished.

had a pub, the Gun on Scotswood Road. John's friend Billy Stokoe played accordion. "We had our wedding do there. One song I remember was *When your old wedding ring was new*. Everybody knew the songs. If someone wanted to sing or play nobody objected or felt embarrassed. Everybody danced – we went to the Oxford. There was a ten piece band with a saxophonist. If you danced near the front of the stage, you couldn't hear your partner speaking it was so loud."

"I bought us a car for £40 and a caravan for £60 from an Irishman who used to take it with him when he worked in Seahouses. We went to Great Yarmouth on holiday with it and on the way back coming through Gateshead, the exhaust came off. We were stopped by a policeman. When he saw the kids in the back, he said "For goodness sake just get home as quick as you can!"

John recalls other jobs that he enjoyed. "Everywhere I went I met new people. I fixed car radiators at Sercks on Skinnerburn Road right at the bottom near the river. I also worked with the regional comedians such as Bobby Hooper and his mate. One played the straight role and the other one was funny. When I worked on the fruit and veg market, he was the salesman. I took the goods on barrows to the front. Traders came from the shops to collect them. I started work at five in the morning. There were no trams until 5.30 am so I walked from Elswick. The hours were five until two, five and a half days a week. Only the half day was five till one, not really a half day! Some of them gave a tip which was known as the "Bung". Some of them hid until I disappeared, you had to fight for it and follow them all over. I only got £6 a week wages."

John took up drawing and painting in his 60s. He began when he was living on Armstrong Road. "I went into hospital for a hip replacement operation. I was put into a cot, but while still under the anaesthetic I imagined that I was in the ladies' ward and I tried to climb out. I fell to the floor and ripped all of the wires inside my hip, it all had to be done again. When I got home I was upstairs and stayed still for a while, but having always been active I tried to get downstairs. Then, sure enough, I fell again and the same thing happened. I decided to stay put after that and one day I was watching an Italian American woman teaching painting on television. I bought all of the equipment and eventually made quite a good job of it. When I think back to when I was a kid – I used to draw people with little heads and big bodies like the cigarette cards, so I must have always had it in me. I went to a class at the Denton Burn Association where the bowling green is outside. I used to hold my own class for the disabled at Shafto Court where I live – flowers, landscapes and all sorts of things."

John is proud of his achievements in his art works. He is pictured at West End Library with some of his collection.

He looks back on his life when he lived in Scotswood. He smiles as he remembers. "Them days in Scotswood, everyone knew everyone else. Everyone married people from within the community and there was always family and neighbours for support. If any kid stepped out of line there was always someone to stop and say "Hi, I'll tell your mother!" When they started to demolish the area, aunties, grandparents, brother, sisters were sent to places like Westerhope, Blakelaw, Fenham – all over the place. And that is when the problems started, there was nobody to look out for the kids."

John is always seen in and around Benwell. He attends Slatyford Lane Day Centre. At one time there were over twenty members with different activities offered every day. "There are only six of us now, people have left over the years – I hope that more people will join. I was going to teach them how to make clippy mats. There are amateur painting groups where you do your own thing – it's a drop in with tea and scones."

John and Ann fostered children and took in a fair few over the years. The couple have a plaque from the council acknowledging their support. He credits his good upbringing to the caring ways of his mother. "I think that I had a good childhood and my mam always looked after me and everyone else around her. It rubbed off on me, that's why I like to make sure everyone's ok."

Shows, Shopkeeping and Strays
by Elsie Moore

Elsie Moore was born at 64 Greenhow Place in 1918. Her granny was born at the top of Maughan Street and during this time Greenhow Terrace and Greenhow Place were just being built. Elsie's mother told her that back then when babies were born everyone helped. "Everyone took on a job and money was never mentioned. It didn't cost you anything to have a baby in those days – someone baked, did the washing, someone else took on the ironing and so on. The young mother was well looked after. Mam baked on Tuesdays and I went to Mrs Taylor's with cake and bread for her. She made broth and we shared. It came in a huge jug. There was an old lady who used to hang out of the window watching everything that was going on in the street from morning until night. We used to call it "tooting."

Elsie spoke about an old pal who she enjoyed spending her time with. "Norman Carr lived next door to us, he lived with his granny. I remember that his uncle worked for White Horse Whisky and he used to bring little horses badges home, he gave me some. They were the only family in the street who had a phone. One day he was going to play golf and he left us sitting in the car. It had one of those little dicky seats at the back which could be folded away. We began sliding down it, we didn't think to take our buckled shoes off and it was all scratched. He went mad when he saw

Elsie Moore.

the damage we had done, we were only about seven years old. Norman and I had started school together at South Benwell. Teachers I remember were Mr Hall, Mr Matthews and I think there was also a Miss Hall."

"Dad had worked as a plumber for Swan's, but he was out of work for a while. I was sent home with a letter from school. Mam opened it. It said that anyone whose dad was out of work could claim free dinners and books. She wouldn't hear of claiming and threw the letter in the bin. We weren't too badly off, some boys at the school went without boots. After school we all ran home to play. We used to enjoy watching the big lads playing montakitty, but really, the back lane was split into two. The lads kicking balls and the lasses skipping."

"My mam bred canaries when we lived at Greenhow Place. When you turned the corner of the street you could hear them. My aunt Meggy lived in West View – she had a parrot and I loved to go up there to see it. It sang *Half a Pound of Tuppenny Rice*. I used to walk along Bournemouth Terrace (which was later renamed as Buddle Road). Back then there were no kerb stones on that road and I used to walk my nana along there. I was only four and she was blind, but it was a straight run, no traffic and we walked as far as the

Elsie Moore with her son Johnny on her knee. Elsie was one of the smartest ladies in the area.

chemist at the corner of Maria Street. All of the gardens were lovely with railings around, but the metal was used for the war effort."

Elsie attended dance lessons at the home of Florence Leithead on Bournemouth Terrace. Ballet was performed on Fridays, ballroom dancing on Saturday. "We also did tap dancing. There was no stage work then only pantomimes. In 1930 I was in *Babes in the Wood* at the Majestic and in 1931 in *Red Riding Hood*. I left school in 1932 and met May Danskin in one of the pantomimes. I used to go to the Paramount (Odeon) there were two main films and, in between the films, there was a stage show. It was run by the two Miss Terry's and it was called Terry's Juveniles. Most of the cast were from London. I begged my mam to take me to an audition. She said that dad wouldn't let me, I was only fourteen, but I got there anyway. Me and my pal May went along and one of the Miss Terry's asked us what we could do and we showed her. She said she'd contact us in a couple of weeks. When me and mam got outside she turned to me and said "Well, that's it, we'll never hear from her." However, we did get the job. There were forty interviewees and eight of us were picked. I got twelve shillings and sixpence a week, about fifty three pence today. We were given food and accommodation as we travelled all over the country with the troupe. We went to Portsmouth, Aberdeen, Birmingham and Southsea. It was a big part of my life. I was earning more than my dad. But when we performed near home either my mam

Elsie's mam and dad – John Birrell and Grace Amelia Newstead – taken in 1912 just before they were married.

or May's mam took us there. I remember one of the shows was called *Whitehorse Inn*."

Elsie returned to Newcastle after working on a show. "When I got to the Newcastle Central Station I saw my dad waiting for me. He told me not to get upset, but mam was in the General Hospital having gallstones removed. I was in the show until I was sixteen and then I got a job at the Co-op in town. I had to walk to work and I was paid ten shillings a week. I loved working there but one day I came home from a shift and mam told me that she had got me a job at Vickers. I started to cry, I didn't want to go there, but it was the lead up to the war and they were paying £2 a week. My dad also got a start at Vickers and by then I was earning more than him for the second time. I worked on an ammunition machine and a lady from the bond came to watch me to check that I was doing it properly. I used to put a wire into the fuse and tap it to get the right tension. We worked from 7.30 am until 7.30 pm to earn £2."

"I remember listening to May's mam talking about her children. She was saying that twenty one had been born and all to the same father. Her husband was a little pitman. One of their sons was killed in the Montagu Pit disaster, we just knew him as Ginger Danskin."

While working for Vickers, Elsie met Edna

This photo shows Elsie's mam on Buddle Road which had previously been known as Bournemouth Terrace. The baby is Grace Amelia Birrell.

Potts who lived on Pease Avenue. She was to become a lifelong friend. "We were both working on ammunition. Her husband was badly injured by machine gun fire while serving in Burma. He had been a plumber by trade before the war. He opened a shop because he couldn't continue with his trade because of his injuries. Edna always held a party every Christmas Day. Their son Ian became one of the head men of the London School of Economics. I got married in 1939 during the outbreak of war. Reggie was in the army and had forty eight hours leave. Our reception was at the Rex Hotel in Whitley Bay. I wore a dress, coat and hat."

A typical children's party with everyone seated at the table. Notice the lacy tablecloth and cake stands. Johnny Moore is seen near the window.

Elsie and Reggie lived at no 42 Third Avenue in Heaton. Elsie and Reggie bought a shop at 110 Maria Street that stood at the corner of Maria and Buddle Road. "My mam helped in the shop – Johnny was born at number 40 Third Avenue in Heaton in 1947. When we moved to the shop at Maria Street, he attended South Benwell School then on to Atkinson Road. He took part in the Red Spot Babies project which has tracked the progress of children in our area. Peter was born in 1951 he attended South Benwell School and went on to John Marley."

She quickly formed friendships with locals. "I had a good friendship with Gladys Bonner and I loved her two daughters Olive and Gladys. I used to say "Where's little Glad?" She used to take our Pepi the poodle out for walks. Edie Jones organised the trips to the coast. Mary Brown was a big noble lass, nobody dare set about her kids when she was there. I always left the door open on New Year's Eve and all the customers came in. Our front door was up about six steps onto Maria Street. I remember one year it was thick of snow and you couldn't see the steps. Freddie Bonner was on his way out with a pal, we took them to the front door. They both had a Woodbine in their hands and they bumped right to the bottom, but they didn't drop their tabs. We always kept cats and the customers used to laugh when they came into the shop, there'd be a few of them sitting on the newspapers. They had to move them out of the way to pick up their paper. Since I was 32, I've counted the stray cats I've taken in; Jimmy, Blackie, Tiger, Thomas, Jack, Kitty and Millie."

Another couple took over the shop next door and Reggie and Elsie went on day trips together every Sunday afternoon to the Yorkshire moors. "Jennie Spry came to work in our shop, she had previously worked in Gordon Wilson's shop and as we were looking towards having more time off from our business, we took her on. She's 90 years old now and is regularly on the telephone to me."

The hours were long when Elsie and Reggie ran the shop. "We were open at 6 am. Our Peter was always running all over the place. He knew all the workmen. He was only about three years old. His pals were Tommy and Phil Simons. I remember when he was about nine years old he asked to sleep over at the Simons house. I said that he couldn't, but Reggie said

Peter Moore and Johnny Hewitt on the roof of the family shop. Notice the road sweeper going past.

that he could. When I opened the door the next day, he was sitting on the step. "I couldn't sleep," he said. Peter used the cellar of the shop as a base for his band the Bluebeats to practise. He loved the Beatles music, but he was too young to stand in the queue for tickets to see them. Our Johnny went with John Cross for tickets. When they came back, John asked me "Have you ever seen anyone falling asleep against a wall?"

Local kids congregated around the Moore's corner shop, especially when the Bluebeats were playing. Band members were Peter, Joe May, Dave Anderson and Bobbie Barton who went on to play with Beckett.

"One day a lass came into the shop with a sixpence. She asked for change, two three penny bits. I asked her why she needed change and she replied "To get into the cellar." I went storming down there. Our Peter was charging an admittance fee of three pence. He said that Reggie had asked for money for all of the electricity the band were using."

Elsie took up dancing again when Peter was eighteen. "I enjoyed modern sequence dancing. It was to last for 25 years. I went to church halls – the Milvain and Denton Burn Social Club among lots of other places. I remember Lily White was everywhere I went. She always wore lovely clothes. I was 82 when I was on the way back from a dance with my pal June on the bus. I got off at near the Rington's Tea building near Shields Road and I thought, "I'll have to give this up, I'm too tired." June still comes to see me every week, she's 76 now."

As I'm talking to Elsie, her granddaughter Kay is hoovering, putting on the washing machine and preparing a meal for her. She makes a cup of tea for us and sits down for a chat. Kay is Johnny's daughter and she and partner Darren have one son, Charlie. There are photos of Charlie on every wall among other family pictures. We go through her photos and she tells me how lucky she is to have such a good family. "They really look after me. Our Johnny lives nearby with Jan, he comes here every morning at 7.30 am before he starts work for a cup of tea and Kay is here every day cooking my dinner. Peter and Susan also visit for a chat and we sometimes have days out."

Kay makes us another cup of tea before she leaves and tells her gran that Spaghetti Bolognaise is ready for when she needs it. When I go into the kitchen to wash our cups, there is a tray set out with a cup with a tea bag and sweetener inside, a knife, fork and napkin at the ready. On my way out, Elsie shows me her cat Millie, who has been absent throughout my visit, she's curled up in the bottom of the wardrobe. "I've got two little huts in the back yard where I feed the strays. I love this house and I'll never move from here."

Peter at the back and in front are left to right: Gary Craig, John Rolfe and Trevor Jones. The photo was taken around 1963. These were the original members of the band, the Bluebeats, and a fifth member was Jimmy Lowes who joined when he came back from Australia. Peter remembers before he owned drums he used biscuit tins and the symbols were the lids.

Our Roots Are Still In Elswick
by Tom and Stanley Dawson

Tom and Stanley Dawson were born half an hour apart. Tom came at 11.45 pm and Stan at 12.15 am on the 10th and 11th of July 1925. The place of birth was 3 Marsden Street, Elswick. Their parents were Thomas Stanley and Anne. The family lived above the shop of which they were owners. It was a general dealers and off beer license which wasn't very profitable. "There was a fair bit of unemployment at the time," said Stanley. "Most of the people were honest and did their best to pay for the goods that they needed. We remember an elderly widow who brought her clock over for us to keep as temporary payment for goods if she had no money. The next week, she returned with the money, an honest lady."

Mrs Dawson standing outside her shop on Marsden Street with Beaumont Street flats in the background.

The twins had three older sisters, Mabel, Joyce and Marjorie who all got on well together. "We used to spend a lot of time at Elswick Park. It was a very popular place where people played bowls and tennis. On other occasions, we went to Nunsmoor Park under the watchful eyes of our Mabel."

Tom and Stanley were at Elswick School in 1930 until 1937. Both boys passed exams which enabled them to go to Atkinson Road Technical School. "We had a happy time at that school. Teachers who we remember were Mr Gair, Mr Douglas, Mr Scott, Mr Brooks and Mr Wright. But, at the beginning of 1939, war was declared and we were evacuated to Workington, Cumberland which is now known as Cumbria. Our home for the next eleven months was with a lady who ran a boarding house. It did take a little while for us to settle into our new surroundings. Some of the time was spent in makeshift accommodation like a spare room in a Masonic lodge."

Stanley and Tom recall that they were given a good education there and they amused themselves with musical interludes. Stan played the harmonica. "We always enjoyed these impromptu sessions. Eventually we settled in at Workington Technical School which was just next door to where we were living. Our mother and sisters used to come from Newcastle once a month to see us. We left school in July 1940 and returned home. Both of us started work for Vickers Armstrong, Scotswood Works and began our apprenticeships as fitters. We worked in what was known as 11 Shop and worked on 3.7" anti-aircraft guns. Our dad was a charge hand and he certainly didn't offer us any favours, in

Tom on the left and Stanley to the right outside their door on Atkinson Road. Nobody would guess that the boys were twins.

fact he made sure that we toed the line much more than the other apprentices."

Their dad was also on ARP (Air Raid Precautions) as a warden. He was expected to be on call if there was a raid by German bombers. "One night during an incendiary bomb raid, St Michael's Roman Catholic Church on Westmorland Road was set on fire. The roof was well alight and our Tom went out and helped the priest with others to carry out various valuables. Dad heard about this later and Tom got a ticking off as he shouldn't have gone out in the first place."

Early in 1946 Tom and Stanley were called up into the forces.

Stanley looks on as his boss gives instructions to an apprentice at Vickers.

"Tom joined the RAF and became a PT instructor while I joined the Royal Corps of Signals in the army. After early training I was posted to Germany and I went to Palestine."

In 1948, both of them were demobbed and returned to civilian life. "For several years Tom had been very keen on gymnastics and was a member of the Vickers Armstrong Apprentice Welfare Gymnastic Team. He became so proficient that in 1952 he just missed out on being selected for the Olympic Games. He was so close to representing Great Britain in Helsinki at his chosen sport."

Stan was first to marry and moved to Wallsend. Tom married later and lived in Gateshead. In the early 1970s Marsden Street was demolished. "The street we had grown to love was no more. We both still felt that our roots were entrenched in Elswick."

In the Vicker's gym with Tom balancing on the bars.

Right: I took this photo of Tom and Stanley in 2010. We were on our way to Atkinson Road School to attend a reunion. This year the school celebrates its centenary.

Californian Poppy, Aqua Manda and Evening in Paris
by Val Clift (née Chalmers)

Val Chalmers was born in 1939 at Phillip Street opposite Featonby's the bakers on the corner of Beaconsfield Street. One of ten children, her siblings were Alan, Janet, Ian, Dougie, Ray, Terry, Alfie, Marnie and Royston. She attended Todd's Nook School. Her dad worked at the CWS bacon factory on Blandford Street. Brother Alan became a driver on the trolley buses. She remembers the pork shop on Elswick Road where the Ponderosa is now, it used to be a row of shops. Just around the corner stood the Portland.

"Gibson's Fruit Shop stood at the corner of Meldon Street. They sold the biggest cooking apples I had ever seen. A hardware shop sold sticks and firelighters for the fire and I loved going in there. The staff would ask me what I wanted to buy and I said I've just come in for a smell. Even now if there is an aroma which reminds me of that shop my memories take me back. They sold San Isal, a kind of Dettol. I loved the smell of tar on the roads when it was being put down. I used to go to the fish shop at the bottom of Malvern Street. The Woodbine Laundry was at the top of Northbourne Street, there are flats there now. Sister Margaret worked there, we used to take our washing and dry cleaning there. James Street carried on to a pub – the Independent – a post office and a pawn shop further along. If I took newspapers to McMoran's fish shop, I got a free bag of chips. Mrs Ritson worked at Ridsdales at the corner of Stanton Street and Fenham Road. I used to put out the empty Puroh bottles into the crates for her, I got one penny for that job. I got three pennies to go for a message."

Val remembered that she also ran errands for an old lady who lived in Beaconsfield Street. "My dad used to look out of the window and as we lived near the shops he'd let me know if anyone needed me. We had a nickname for the old lady as she only ever needed me to get snuff for her. Dad would say "Here's Buckeye Snuff for you." Or "Mrs

Northbourne Street before demolition.

Ritson is waving for you to put crates out."

"We did all sorts. My sister Janet and me used to go Christmas carolling and shovelling snow along Wingrove Road and Moorside North. Sometimes we looked through the windows, they were lovely houses. Mrs Stephenson organised trips on Beaconsfield Street and she helped out during the Coronation street party. I left Phillip Street when I was 14 years old."

Val's mother loved going to the Brighton Cinema to watch Norman Wisdom films. She enjoyed his song *Don't Laugh at me 'cos I'm a Fool*. Val and Janet had to be back in the house by 9 pm. If they were late, they would be in trouble. "If we were late and we ran to the front door, Janet always ran back to shut the gate, leaving me to get the blame because I was older and dad said that I should know better."

Val wore her hair in the Bridgette Bardot style and sometimes tied it in a long pony tail then wrapped it around her head. She loved wearing perfume. "There was a house nearby in Philip Street, the woman kept her windows sparkling clean so after I'd had my hair cut I could check how it looked in the glass before me and Janet went to school. The lads (Val's brothers) went to Dickie James barbers on Stanhope Street. We used to go to the market to buy Lavender. There was a little chemist shop which used to be a cafe. We bought Californian Poppy, Aqua Manda and Evening in Paris then go to the dance once a week and hoy the lot on ourselves. Evening in Paris came in a lovely bottle, one half was silver and the other half dark blue. It only cost a few coppers. Pan stick makeup was fashionable, but I only wore lipstick. I wore stockings with diamantes up the back during the Elvis Presley era. There were Teddy Boys everywhere."

"I listened to Winnie Atwell on Sunday Radio, we had to have the battery charged up every Saturday. I enjoyed listening to Michael Miles when he asked the contestants if they wanted to take the money or open the box. If the contestants opened the box we laughed when someone won a booby prize."

The Elswick baths and police station which stood across the road from St Stephen's Church. Val remembers the imposing baths building which was also used as a wash house.

She remembered going up to Ponteland on a trailer during the summer holidays. "We collected a pail of tea before we started. It was seven and sixpence and sometimes two and sixpence for picking tatties. A horse and plough churned the soil up first and we held our pinnys by the four corners to collect the potatoes. The farmer came to collect them and we were given one bag free to take home. It was good sitting on the bales of hay at dinner time. The earnings all went straight to my mother. Sometimes we went turnip "snadging". We didn't get sweets very often, we ate pea pods, they were sweet. People had healthy teeth back then, but if you needed teeth pulled there was a little clinic in the back lane of Lynwood Avenue. After we left Phillip Street we moved to Cowgate."

Val was married in 1959 to Harry Clift. Harry and his family had lived at 2 Park Road. Harry's dad used to be a boxer and Val used to go over the road to Caspers Bar to bring him a jug of beer. The family all attended Bethany Hall Church which stood opposite the house. Harry also sang at the church and his two sisters Jean and Lily were married there. Val and Harry moved to a flat at Beech Grove Road. "The flat had one bedroom and we had to share a bathroom with everyone else. There were six families. The Dixon's were downstairs and the McGuires. When we were first married, Harry worked on opencast so he got up at 6 am. It was a standing joke that I wasn't any good at cooking because when I'd been at home everything was done for me. They used to say "She can't even cook an egg." The eggs used to explode. I used to put the potatoes on in the morning and leave them on all day continually topping up with water. The potatoes just disappeared. One thing I could make was Cadbury's Smash!

When I was expecting my first baby, I used to go for a bath to my mam's house or to the Scotswood Road baths where I put six pence in the meter."

She laughs as she remembers an astracan coat with a fox fur collar which was bought for her on £100 ticket and Harry got a leather coat. "Harry was mad on bikes. He took my coat down to Ken's Motorcycles on Scotswood Road and swapped it for motor bike. He got a straight exchange for the coat. I was livid at the time. He used to take them to bits in the attic. He was always messing about with bikes. We also owned a motorbike and sidecar. He had a pal, Jimmy Dixon who was a painter and decorator, he used to take on wallpapering for people. I remember that he wallpapered ceilings and always wore a white overall. Another friend of Harry's was Terry Walls, he was a teddy boy who wore a camel Crombie coat, they all wore them. Harry was also pals with Sunnie Leonard, the boxer who lived on Park Road."

Harry Clift looking smart wearing his trendy knitted tie with letter H on the front.

"I had never been allowed to go to dances before I was married, but I did go to the Oxford Galleries with Harry where we danced the Bradford Barn. We also used to go for a game of Bingo. Back then we played on a board with beer bottle tops for the dobbers. I used to run down there to get a free game, sometimes you got a bit sugar with your vouchers with what you won at the Bingo."

Val worked at various trades. She worked at the Co-op on Newgate Street, Sarah Gaskins, flowers in the market, the Rialto Cinema at Gosforth, Norbrit's Shoe Factory which was near the Telegraph pub in Orchard Street. They made all of the teddy boy's shoes with diamantes. Harry was a skilled workman who worked at Jepson's Cranes on dismantling, in Scotland as a steel erector and on opencast at Heddon on the Wall, he also put tar down on the roads. Harry had his own business at one time called Harry

Val and Harry pictured on the right on a night out at the pub.

Clift Compressors – the building was on Hanover Street and was used in the Catherine Cookson film *The Gambling Man*. He also had premises in Mill Lane and Gateshead – the business was successful until he died. Harry enjoyed a drink or two at the Cushy Butterfield pub on a Sunday morning. He went to the Pine Street Club to play Bingo. Val didn't go along very often, but when she did she sang *I don't know why I love you but I do* by Clarence Frogman Henry. Other pubs around there were the Rock, the Globe on Railway Street and the Chesterfield which later became the Independent.

"We used to go to the Fish Quay and

put herring in the bath to keep them fresh when we lived at Cowgate. Harry's mother was a cook at Grainger Park School. She used to bring wiliks back from North Shields, boil them and put them in a bag with a pin at the corner. They were sold for 6d a bag. It used to keep the kids occupied, the time it took them to take the eyes out. Lovely with some salt and vinegar. We went to Kettlewell's in the Grainger Market for our fishcakes."

"There were some dramas, Harry jnr was born in Dilston Hall, the first bairn. I was on the back of Dougie Chalmers moped when my waters broke. Then, when I was having Lloyd, I walked up Beech Grove Road to call the Doctor. When I told him that my waters had broken in the telephone box he asked "Well what are you doing there, go home?"

Harry and Lloyd were born in Beech Grove Road, Vincent and Tyrone born at 2 Crown Street, Sterling; Earl and Christon at Ash Street; Sam was born at 68 Malvern Street and the other children Carmen, Solomon, Simon, Leon, Courtney, Crystal and Spencer were all born while the family lived at Cowgate. Some of the children attended Ashfield Nursery, Westgate Hill School, Rutherford School and Montague School. Nearly all of Harry and Val's children were christened at Bond Street Church on Adelaide Terrace in Benwell. Some of the children went to West Parade Nursery which was on the corner of Westmorland Road and West Parade. They attended Westgate Hill School. The others attended Rutherford College.

Harry Clift outside his premises on Hanover Street which was used by the film crew for Catherine Cookson's 'The Gambling Man'.

They have a family rhyme known by all of the family is. When Val was at her hen do from Norbrit's Shoes the staff wrote this rhyme on her back when she left to get married.

> *One Chalmers less*
> *One Clift more*
> *In years to come*
> *Clift's galore*

Sam her daughter said "They weren't far wrong there were they?"

From Walker to Benwell
by George Melrose

George Melrose was born 6th September 1947 at the Princess Mary Maternity Hospital, Jesmond. "At that time my parents George Melrose snr and Jane (née Dunn) Melrose were living in with her parents, Tommy and Jane Dunn at 16 Walker Road, Byker. When I was three years old, we moved to 55 Hugh Gardens, Benwell. My father George was an engineer's machinist at Vickers. He was born at Buddle Road in 1918. His parents James and Margaret lived at Buddle Road. My dad was one of six brothers, James, William, Robert, Stan and John and four sisters, Mary, Margaret, Elizabeth and Frances."

George Melrose Snr in Vickers Machine Shop around 1950s.

George played football in the back lane after school and at weekends. "We enjoyed going to the Majestic Cinema where we watched Laurel and Hardy, the Three Stooges, Flash Gordon and numerous westerns, always giving a rousing cheer when the cavalry appeared! My mother was friendly with two sisters who lived on Clara Street – Nora Webb and Evelyn Turner. Their father had a cottage at Sparty Lea, Allendale and one year, my parents and I went up there for our summer holidays. Although the cottage had no amenities and was very basic, we were allowed to work on the farm gathering the hay. It was my first taste of the countryside and it was one of the best holidays I have ever had. Years later I went up there to try to pinpoint where it had stood, but couldn't."

George started at Atkinson Road Infants School in September 1952. "I went on to Atkinson Road Juniors, and Secondary Modern in 1957. When I was twelve or thirteen years old I joined the 25th Boys' Brigade, Atkinson Road which was connected to Sopwith Street Mission. Basically, I joined there to get the belt and hat, but after a few weeks I lost interest. Mr Lockhart knocked at our front door to ask for them back. Then after another few weeks I went back again. This went on for some time, but Mr Lockhart

This photo was taken in the school yard at Atkinson Road in 1961. Back row, left to right: Mr Stockdale (Sports teacher), John Cross 5th boy along. Front row: Rob Varley, Ronnie Johnson, Ray McFee, Les Baptist, George Melrose.

The 25th Boys' Brigade at Atkinson Road in 1959. It was connected to Sopwith Street Mission. Front row, left to right: Eddy Clifford, ?, Lenny Williamson, Mr Lockhart, George Sewell, ?, Ray McFee. Second row: ?, ?, Robert Kidd, George Melrose, ?, Colin Laing.

always called back for the hat and belt! Like most lads, I thought school was to be endured. I couldn't wait until I was fifteen and I could leave and get a job and some money in my pocket. I never stayed for school dinners as I only had a five minute run along the Pipe Track to get home. In my lunch hour I used to watch the *One O'clock Show* on Tyne Tees Television, then make a mad dash back to school. I always remember I hated Sunday nights after watching *Maverick* on TV. I knew the next day it was back to school and my first lesson was arithmetic!"

George left Atkinson Road School in 1962 and his first job was working in the Co-op Butchers on the West Road. "When I left the butchers I got a job at Electrical Suppliers in Gallowgate, then in 1969 I joined the Post Office. I remained there until I took early retirement in 2004. In 1975 my parents and I finally moved, reluctantly from Hugh Gardens after they started clearance of that part of Benwell. Looking back, they were happy days, despite school. The streets and lanes were our playground where we could stay out till all hours. The neighbours were decent, hardworking people and everyone helped one another. The front doors were always open because let's face it, in those days everyone was in the same boat, they didn't have anything of great value in their homes, so there was nothing to steal!"

This photograph was taken in the back lane at Hugh Gardens in the early 1950s. Left to right: Colin Laing, Norman Laing, Terry Quinn, David Kidd, Robert Kidd, Bobby Turner and George Melrose.

75

Please Hang Up and Try Again Later
by Harry Bennett

Harry Bennett was born in 1927 at 26 Liddle Road, Arthur's Hill. Harry was ten and a half pounds in weight when born. His Dad Henry Wood Bennett was born in 1896 and became a post office telegraphist. "Dad worked at Newcastle head office, St Nicholas Post Office opposite the cathedral, he spent all of his working life in that building. My mam, Jean Elizabeth (née McLure) worked as a telephonist in the same building."

Harry attended Cowgate School on Cypress Avenue. "I was there when it first opened. I remember it being built because at the time I lived at 27 Greenway on the estate opposite Fenham Library. The house is still there. My second school was Rutherford College Boys' School on Bath Lane in town. I met Fred Millican there and we are still pals today. I was only there for one year as I was evacuated to Carlisle. I was away for three years. The headmaster was Mr Maw and Charles Stuart Hall was his successor in 1939. I got into trouble when I was running down the last staircase to the ground floor. The door opened and the headmaster came out, he made me walk right back up to the top then walk back down again."

He remembers learning how to swim at Snow Street baths. "Mr Thompson sent me down to the shallow end. I was scared and he said "Lift your feet up and swim." It did the trick and I was ok after that."

Harry Bennett's father Henry and grandmother Rachel are seated in the kitchen of the Brighton Ballroom at Arthur's Hill. Third from the back is Mrs McEuen who lived on Croydon Road. Rachel (née Kennedy) Bennett was catering manageress and mother to Henry Wood and Grandmother to Harry. Extreme right at back of photo is Phyllis Archibold (née Kennedy) who was Rachel Kennedy's niece.

RUTHERFORD COLLEGE BOYS' SCHOOL NEWCASTL

A group photo of pupils at Rutherford High School taken in 1939. Harry is sitting 7th from the left in the front row and Fred Millican 9th from the left of the same row.

After leaving Rutherford, Harry worked for one year as an electrician's apprentice for the Tyne Improvement Commission now Port of Tyne Authority at Albert Edward Dock at North Shields.

"My next job was as a Post Office engineer, I started from Buxton Street near City Road. We had a garage there and a base where all of the engineers who had vans set off from. I replaced the broken bits on telephones, but there weren't many around in those days during the war. I got my leg pulled quite a lot by a guy who I later found out was a ventriloquist. It was nearly a fortnight before I found out; he used to throw his voice behind me and when I looked around there was nobody there. I spent the rest of my career as a Post Office Engineer, forty two and a half years."

"I went to Gosforth telephone Exchange and also to Lemington, which isn't there now. I was working at Bentinck Road West Auto in June 1944 when the announcement was made that we had invaded Normandy. I remember sitting at 9.30 listening to radio and having a cup of tea. There was a terrible clatter and congestion on the lines, all of the rotary equipment was turning. Everyone was trying to make telephone. We had to make announcements asking folks to hang up and try again later. In some cases we switched the power supply off."

Harry was married at Benwell Grove Methodist Church to Margaret Renner in 1955. At the time Margaret had been employed as a GPO telephonist at Carliol House since 1944. She left on being married and didn't go back to work for many years. Their children were John David born 1957, followed by Paul Hamilton 1958, Peter Angus 1960 and David Charles in 1962. David died in 1975 from leukaemia.

Harry still works with his old school pal Fred at West Newcastle Picture History Collection group which is based at West End Library at the bottom of Condercum Road. He scans and records photos which are then placed in the archive at the library.

Parades, Physics and Photos
by Fred Millican

Frederick Douglas Millican was born in 1927. He lived at 77 Gloucester Street. Fred attended Westmorland Road School until he took the entrance examination scholarship. (It wasn't known as the eleven plus at this time.) He went to Rutherford College Boys' School. "I remember Messiur Peugniez who took French – he got Puggy as a nickname and there was Tosh Hindson who took maths and physics. Harry Bennett was in the same class as me and in the past ten years we have resumed our friendship. Mr Thompson was the gym master. Charles Stewart Hall became headmaster on 1st September 1939 – that was the year war broke out. Mr Pringle was my teacher in the fifth form and also my Geography teacher. I remember that I got into trouble for riding to school on my bike with my hands in my pockets as I had no gloves."

Fred went to a Co-op youth club in Buckingham Street. The big Co-op was downstairs so the rooms upstairs were very large. He played table tennis. He went for his hair cut to the barbers in Gloucester Street. "I remember the winters. In 1947 the trams were stuck on Scotswood Road for three days because of severe weather."

Fred's first job was for Vickers Armstrong in 1942 in the laboratory. He was training to become a metallurgist. It involved dealing with metals and heat treatments to make them stronger and also investigating and detecting faults. His bosses were Mr A. Wragg and Mr Jimmy Brown. He attended evening classes until 1948 for four nights a week taking physics, maths, metallurgy and chemistry. "In 1942 I was in the civil defence messenger service. We were based at the Old Police Station at Scotswood Road Depot. I wore a uniform and went on duty with my bicycle. At St James' Park there was a big parade of all the civil defence people, somebody important came but I can't remember who it was."

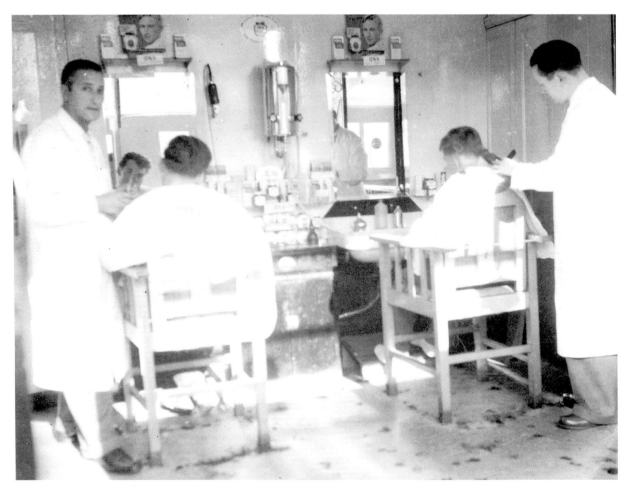

Frank's barbers shop on Gloucester Road in 1957.

These young lads are in charge of the shop horse in 1945. I wonder if they would have time to go to the Co-op club as Fred used to do when he was a young lad.

"On my night off on Mondays I ran Wolf Cubs which were young scouts. It was the 14th Newcastle St Paul's pack for lads aged from eight to eleven years of age. The St Paul's School building was at the top of Victoria Street off Westmorland Road. Activities involved tying knots, games, flags, agility tests and skipping to keep fit. We organised trips up the river."

"A friend of mine who worked at the lab decided to follow teaching as a profession. We both had the qualifications from work at Vickers which enabled us to qualify for the course. I went into training in 1964 at Huddersfield Technical Teachers Training College. I came home at weekends. When I qualified, I taught at Cowgate School. The city was changing to the comprehensive system and I went to Blakelaw Comprehensive School. My pal Bill Chennelles was working there. Later I taught at Sacred Heart Grammar School."

Fred is a member of the West Newcastle Picture History Collection at West End Library and is also involved with the Friends of the Laing Art Gallery. He is still involved with church activities and meetings.

Fred Millican and Mike Young at Des Walton's 90th party which was held at Fenham Library in 2010.

I Always Go Back to Where I Know
By Sharon Glendinning Clarke

Benwell life began for my family way back in 1866 when the Glendinning's arrived for work in the coal industry from Northumberland. My Grandmother Emily Glendinning (née Haswell) was also born in the West End just off Stanhope Street and the picture taken of all the children in the back Street at Jefferson Street shows her as a child (4th from the right of the photo on the right). Emily's father Alexander Haswell had been a crane driver then the local chimney sweep – a profession never wanting for clients, much like that of the local undertakers! The Haswell family later moved to 109 Hugh Gardens in Benwell and Emily now married with a family eventually took over the flat which is where my story begins.

Emily Haswell is pictured 4th from the right. The photo was taken in 1910 on Jefferson Street. The coal hatches can be seen in the background. Coal carts would be driven around the back lanes and the sacks emptied into the hatches.

I was born in March 1955 at Newcastle General Hospital. It had been a difficult time for my 21 year old mother, Jean who went into early labour with me, her first child. Neighbours Ida & Fred Treliving already had a young family, and they were there to give her support when my mam's own mother, who lived in the East End of Newcastle left for the day. Because my dad worked long hours Ida travelled to the hospital in the ambulance when she went into early labour and stayed with her until my dad, Alan Glendinning made his way to the hospital in his work's van. Being a premature baby meant staying in an incubator until my lungs developed enough to breathe on my own and my frail 4lb body weight increased. I was brought back to Hugh Gardens, Benwell, a downstairs 2 bedroom Tyneside flat with sitting room scullery, a back yard and the ubiquitous netty and coal house at the top of the yard. It was a bad winter in Newcastle and central heating didn't exist. We had fires places only in the sitting room and the front bedroom (mam and dad's room) and the rest of the house remained bitterly cold in winter and not much warmer in the summer! It was so cold the condensation would freeze on the inside of your window and the nets would freeze to the window!

The first few weeks of my life was spent wrapped up and tucked in mam's clothes and at night dad's pyjamas to keep me constantly warm according to my mam! Hardship was rife but we never went to bed hungry and your bed always had several layers of blankets and a quilt to keep you warm.

When older I would have a stoneware hot water bottle put in the bed usually wrapped in one of dads vests or a towel so as not get scorched! Eeee, I hated those hot water bottles because you could break your toes on them if you happen to kick out during the night! Often the bung would come out and you would wake up soaked!

My dad, Alan Glendinning worked as an operator fitter at Reed Construction down on Scotswood Road. It was dirty job with long hours, so we would often never see dad from one day to the next because I was in bed before he came home and still asleep when he left at 6 am.

The back yard always had a washing line strewn across and mam would make a game up for me with

Sharon and her sister in the back yard of Hugh Gardens having tea

the household chores. She used to hoy the carpet over the line and give me a wicker carpet beater and let me loose with it! Beating the carpet and choking on the coal dust coming off it was fun! When there was nothing on the line mam would use one of her stocking to make a swing for my doll, tying one end of the stocking to the line and the foot part around the doll's waist. I would spend hours swinging my doll until I was called in for tea. Calling for friends used to be totally different to what you would do today. We used to knock on the door then in a singular elongated pitch shout the name. When friends called for me they would do the same – they would knock then in a single tone sing Shaaaaaarrrrrroooooon!

My sister Janis was born at home in March 1958 in the front bedroom and I remember it was freezing that day. The Midwife made sure the fire in the front bedroom was well banked up throughout mam's labour. I wasn't allowed in the room at the beginning, and when I stood close to the door with my ear pressed to key hole I could feel the heat coming up from under the door. After two smacks and a pitiful cry the door opened and I was allowed in to see my new baby sister who was just being washed in little tin bath in front of the fire. It was a marvellous sight and a moment in time I will always remember. Everyone looked at each other when I asked "Where has she come from?" How the stork got past me without me noticing is beyond me!

Sitting on the front step. Sharon is at the front on the bottom step.

Neighbours in the street were always friendly and such characters! Mr & Mrs Hunter across the road loved dancing and remember some of her ballroom gowns she had were fabulous! It was strange seeing Mrs Hunter hitching the ball gown up to get on at the open back of the number 2 bus wearing stiletto heels and lined stockings and Mr Hunter looking dapper in his Tuxedo and spats! Mr Geggie further down Hugh Gardens used to sit on his step reading the broadsheets and all you could see was a tuft of grey hair and a clenched hand at each end of the paper! The old lady in the house opposite in the back lane (the front of her house would be in Clara Street) would keep old lace for me in the coal house, don't ask me why. I used to go home with this lace and filthy black hands as the old lady would send me in amongst the big chunks of coal to collect the lace. Mam would go mad with me, but I was too polite to refuse it.

When mam sent me for any messages (food shopping), I was sent down to the local corner shop clutching a small snuff box with a ten bob note in it and the change used to be put back in there so I wouldn't lose the money. I always remember my treat was either a jubbly or a sherbet straw which had a scroll of paper in the top and a lucky number written inside. I suppose that was yesterday's version of the lottery lucky dip of today! Sherbet dib dab and spangles were another firm favourite, but believe me – you got them as a treat and not just on demand! You would start your sentence off with, "Can I have" only to be abruptly told "No, you can't!" However, memories of being coaxed to stay in school with 'love hearts' being fed to me through the bars of the school railings at Atkinson Road infants was always an unexpected treat at lunchtime until the yard bell went. The shop on McDonald Road did a roaring trade from the school, and Madge behind the counter always used to put one extra bubbly gum in the packet for being a 'good girl'. The penny glass of pop was treat after school I used to look forward to, and we went to the corner shop opposite the library for that! I would have dandelion and burdock in a little glass for a penny and if you only had a ha'penny the lady would give you half a glass! Better the money in her pocket than yours.

Winter time at school made no difference to your break times – you were 'hoyed oot' to face the elements. I remember in the junior school there was garage type of area under the school building but it had no doors and we all used to congregate in there. The interior had windows but no glass, just bars up looking out onto McDonald Road and a small water fountain which more often than not was frozen up. Stot the ball on the penny was played in the yard and of course skipping, with the lads playing football away from 'the spotty girls'. Pencils were used in class until we reached the juniors when we were allowed a real ink pen to learn how to write with a fountain pen. It was time to do joined up writing! I enjoyed flicking the ink until I was told to stand in the corner. Someone in the class got their own back and put glue onto my seat. I was wearing those horrible navy blue bloomers with a pocket in front and when I tried to get up my knickers were clagged in strings of glue to the seat! I had to be taken with the seat to the toilets to be freed then sent home. The journey up Armstrong Road with glue all over the place was not a pretty site, and very embarrassing!

To help mould me into a young lady I was sent to ballet and tap dancing at Auntie Betty and Uncle Ron's dance group in the scout hut on Atkinson Road opposite the library. I was in quite a few shows – I was a blackbird in one of them and photographers were always on hand for official photos to flog to doting parents.

Pipe Track Lane was a regular haunt for me as I had mates down there. The queue at the chip shop on the corner of Pipe Track Lane seemed to stretch for miles on a Friday night. I used to play two baller against a wall on Pipe Track Lane and was fascinated by the echo of the ball coming from the other walls! Mam used to do her shopping on

Sharon's class taking part in a play – The Blackbird. She is third from the right in the back row.

Adelaide Terrace and the Co-op was the equivalent of today's posh stores. No pre wrapped stuff, there were huge blocks of butter from a cask and tea sold loose into a brown paper packet.

Bath night was not as simple then as it is today. Mam and dad had a large tin bath hung up outside in the back yard. The bath would be brought into the sitting room in front of the fire and hot water brought from the geezer in the scullery by pan and poured into the bath until it was quite full. As I had two sisters by 1959, the baby would be washed first, then Janis and I would share the bath. It didn't end there! When we were put to bed the adults would then take turns in the bath. Emptying it would take ages because the tin bath was that big water had to be ladled out before the bath could be moved. In really bad weather, mam would go to the wash house. I remember the heat from the wooden drying racks was liken to a sauna bath!

We left Benwell in 1962 as a regeneration programme was on the cards and moved to a new brick built semi in Throckley. It was the first time I had seen uninterrupted views of fields and trees instead of cobbled streets and a view of Stella Power Station with its large smoke billowing chimneys. Looking back we had nowt, but we were happy and secure and life was so much simpler and I love going back to the place that I knew and loved.

A Red Spot Baby
by Frank Scott

Frank Scott was born in the Royal Victoria Hospital on 8th June 1947 and was one of the Red Spot Babies. This was a survey of 1,000 children in the West End to assess health issues of families in the area. The study is ongoing and participants are regularly asked to fill in questionnaires and invited to functions to keep up to date with developments. "My house was at number 50 Elswick Row. There were two rooms upstairs and two down with the toilet in the yard. In the winter months it was cold going to the outside toilet with a paraffin lamp as the only light and heating outside. My house had a large room with nine foot high ceilings. At Christmas time, my dad went to the market to buy a tree which reached to the top. Everyone came to our house to see the glass baubles and electric lights. Our house was only one of a few which had both gas and electric lighting. The gas lamps were fitted with mantles which cost four pence each. There was an old fire range oven and a sink."

Hannah (née Shaw) Scott – Frank's grandma. Frank said "It was a time when boy babies were dressed as girls - that's my dad on her knee."

"My granny lived upstairs. There were no hot water taps and we had a boiler in the yard to do the washing in a poss tub. On Mondays, which was wash day, there was a back lane full of clothes on the lines. The rag man came down the lane – we called him Winky Pop. He had a horse and cart and we got a goldfish for the best woollens and a balloon for rags. My brother once got a fish which he exchanged for my granny's cardigan. You can guess what happened! He had to give it back."

"My dad Frank Dominic Scott left school at fourteen years of age. For a time he worked as a stone man at Montagu Pit. To get to work, he caught a tram car to the Fox and Hounds Lane. It turned round at Benwell Hill and went all the way down towards the Denton Hotel. From there he walked to the pit. He joined the army as a volunteer in 1939 a month before the start of the war. On his return from war he was employed by the Breweries, when he left he became a road sweeper for the council in the cleansing department at Newington Road. He cycled to work every day. He worked on the gulley wagons that cleaned the roadside drains by putting a big pipe down and in the winter on the snow ploughs. Sometimes during the winter I never saw him, he'd be out all day and night, shuveling and clearing."

On Buckingham Street there was an old church which was converted to the Gem Picture House. Frank's mother, Frances Ellen Scott worked as an usherette there. The manager was called Big Mac. "She had a torch which she used to show people to their seats. My brother and I sometimes got hold of it to play shining it under the bed clothes. Once, my mam went to use it at work and the batteries had run out. Nowt was the matter the next day when she realised it was us. Batteries were expensive in them days. If we were good we went to the Saturday matinee or we got a comic book – *The Dandy*, *Beezer* or the *Eagle* with Dan Dare, Pilot of the Future. The first big picture I saw was at

Frank as a lad sitting on the wall with his dad at Waverley Terrace. His dad is wearing his demob suit. The Old Rutherford School building is in the background.

the Essoldo, we were given 3-D glasses as we walked in to see *Broken Arrow*. It was great at that time my mam and dad took us there. She also worked for a time at MacKay's Breweries – we used to get bottles of ginger beer and pop."

Frank attended St Mary's Infants School in Bath Lane. "I can always remember the first day at school, I didn't know where I was going – hadn't been informed about it. My mam and dad spoke to the headmistress and all I could smell was sour milk. I could see the milk crates with little bottles all stacked up next to the radiators. They just left me there, and that was it – I was at school. My teacher was called Miss Formister. My best friend there is still my best friend and he was my best man – Donald McIntyre. I used to enjoy going with a friend who lived in Bath Lane to see the blacksmith at work. He worked in the rag shop shoeing horses at the bottom of Corporation Street opposite Rutherford Grammar School. On one of these visits there were thousands of people there. At the time, I didn't know the reason for this, but later found out that it was the Newcastle football team returning with the FA Cup in 1952.

Supporters flocked to see the return of Newcastle's FA Cup winning team in 1952.

He remembers that his first reading book was *The Little Red Hen* which his mother bought him from the Northern School Furnishings in Grainger Street. The price was two shillings. At the age of seven, Frank joined Elswick Library. "The first book I borrowed was all in colour about the planets, but I was only allowed to keep it for four weeks. Sometimes in the summer we went with my granny to Elswick Park where there was a paddling pool. After school I used to go to meet my dad after his work at the brewery. One day I was with my granny on one of these visits – it was around dinner time. While we were standing at the entrance, two large horses were pulling the beer barrel cart. One of them slipped on the cobbled road; kicked my granny breaking her ankle. I also used to watch the men making the beer barrels. They put red hot metal rings over the wooden lathes and a young lad had the job of pouring water over causing lots of steam."

"In Elswick Row there were only a few kids to play with in the back lane. Elswick Street had been demolished and the only remains left were piles of rubble which had overgrown with grass and weeds which was great to play on. Lighting in the back lane was only gas. There were three of them and the one in the middle had a rope tied around one of the metal bars. The bars were used to prop a ladder against so that the glass could be cleaned or the mantles changed. We used to swing on the rope. In the winter, going to school in the mornings, we'd see a sheet of ice on the ground as someone's pipes had burst and the water spread across the lane. It was great for sliding on!"

"Havelock Street was at the bottom of my street where St Paul's, a large church, stood. We enjoyed waiting for the Hoy Oot after weddings where we scrambled for the coins. Also at christenings we were sometimes given a scone with a silver coin inside. We rushed to the corner shop to spend the money on "bullets" (sweets). Every house had a gas meter which you had to put an old penny into. Every now and again the gas man would call to empty it. He always had a large leather bag which he carried over his shoulder. Sometimes I overheard my granny say "Number so and so's have been broken into!""

"I also went to the Green Market in Newgate Street. It always smelled lovely with fresh garden vegetables and garden plants. People were allowed to sell cats and dogs back then. They also sold pigeons for half a crown, but they always flew back to the market. Robinson's Pet Shop was in Clayton Street, we liked going to look at the animals in there. My dad always took us down to Grainger Street once a year to watch the approach of the Circus making its way to the Town Moor for Race Week. I went to the Hoppings with friends from Elswick and spent all day there. Other places we went to were Leazes Park and the Exhibition Park, occasionally to the Brandling Park on the North Road."

"One day I was on my way to play at Summerhill Park when I saw a group of men with sticks. They were trying to catch two bulls which had escaped from the cattle market at Marlborough Street. It was great, everyone running around in a panic. Sometimes dad took me and my brother there, market day was on Mondays."

Frank attended St Mary's Junior School and St Aloysius. His dad also attended St Aloysius and as was the case with many children at the time, he passed his 11 + exam, but was unable to take up the

Frank next to his dad's bike on Elswick Row – Rye Hill can be seen in the background. His mam and dad, Frances and Frank, are standing on the pavement.

position at grammar school because of lack of family funds. Frank talked about the Elswick flats which backed onto the Big Lamp cemetery. Victims of the plague had been buried in the graveyard. He remembered other buildings in the area. "I remember the Blue Man pub, the Hadrian's Arms was its proper name and it was near the graveyard. The council built a public toilet into the wall of the cemetery. I never went in there, I was always scared, I imagined that the skeletons would come out. When I walked along Westgate Road towards the Big Lamp there was a drinking font also in the cemetery wall, it had a big metal cup on a chain. The wall was about twelve feet high and it went the full length of Elswick Street. It had three lights against the wall. My dad told me that the stones had come from the Roman Wall. As kids we never played in the cemetery street, it was a no go area. I recall that there was a big policeman's shed on the corner. There was a frog on the lamp post (switching gear for buses). It was opposite Buchanan's Sweet Shop just before Summerhill Terrace. The bus driver pulled the lever and it went along Elswick Road."

"My brother Kenneth had his tonsils out at the Ear, Nose and Throat Hospital. The building stood at the junction of Westmorland Road and Rye Hill. My mam paid one pound ten shillings for my brother Peter to attend a nursery at West Parade and I had to collect him every night before 5 pm. He was six and a half years younger than me. He used to get a Mars bar or a Five Boys chocolate bar which I was given the money to

The Ear, Nose and Throat Hospital which was later taken over by the College of Arts and Technology. The sandbags outside suggest this photograph was taken during the war.

buy. Guess who got half? Great times. I remember watching a bi-plane and a single wing plane flying over Newcastle advertising Pepsi-Cola. My mam got vouchers and we handed them in to Lawson's Grocers corner shop and we got free bottles, they were red and white. We took the lids off with a tin opener. It was great – I'd never had cola before. We used the metal corks which had a cork seal at the back – took the cork out. We attached the cork lid to our shirt by means of inserting the cork back into the back of the lid and wore them as badges. We did the same with Guinness and Brown Ale bottles."

"When I lived at Elswick Row, I used to go along to Buckingham Street Co-op to put the order in for the shopping. The building is now used by M & C Motorcycles. One side of Elswick Row backed onto Campbell Street back lane and Cromwell Street after that. At the top end of our street was the junction of Westgate Road, the Queen's Arms on the left side coming up from Elswick Road. John Bardgett's undertakers faced Elswick Row on the West Road. The Balmoral is still there and has being refurbished with a new name. There was an archway adjoining to the back lane with a house on top of it."

Frank enjoyed playing in the park on Summerhill Terrace. "The park was opposite St Anne's Convent School. Tramps used to knock on the door to ask for soup. It was near Rye Hill and the allotments went all of the way down. At the time Elswick Road to Westmorland Road was flanked by huge bill boards so that you couldn't see the plants. West Parade was split by the allotments into Belgrade Terrace. After that you had the home for unmarried mothers on Gloucester Road where the tanks went up. St Phillip's Church stood at the corner."

"The tall Todd's Nook flats were built on prefab housing land right across the road from the Snow Street Baths. I remember on my first visit to the pool, I went there on my own wearing my new jacket which I had just got for Easter. I looked through the glass doors and the bottom of the pool was all rusty. When I got back home, my mam asked me why I didn't have my new jacket on. I rushed back, but it hadn't been handed in."

Frank used to go to Mark Toney's ice cream parlour. He remembers the Numol building nearby and Posssinger's Shoe Shop. "My dad witnessed a murder in the area. It was when he was on his way home from the Central Station on leave from the army. The trial lasted six weeks at the Moot Hall and Detective Hetherington was in charge of the case. He came to talk to me and my brother Kenneth and he took us to school to protect our safety. We had a ride in the only police car with a little bell on the front where the bumper bar was. It came from Arthur's Hill police station."

"I remember when they built the Elswick Flats on the old Elswick Street, they were Wimpy constructions. The flats were next to the cemetery and a kid who lived there vandalised the gravestones. They had moved from Loadman Street. Many people whose homes looked onto the Elswick Flats put broken bottles cemented onto the tops of the yard walls to prevent thieves climbing over. I also was around when Todd's Nook flats were going up. A man was injured in the foundations of the middle block. He was working on the seams of an old pit under there and there was a bad accident. It was about 1957 and Todd's Nook flats were being built around then. We moved to Denton Burn around 1958. There were seventeen houses built in a square in Sandmere Place, surrounded by bungalows. You entered into it down Muswell Hill along Yewcroft Avenue. Everybody could trust their neighbours, the same people lived there for years, from 1958-1971."

"On bonfire night everyone had bangers or Roman Candles that fired balls of colour. My best fireworks were called Jumpy Jacks. They seemed to last for ages and cost two pence. Large bangers were two pence or a penny, Roman candles three pence. Bonfires used to stink of the old rubbish that people kept until bonfire night – old beds, mattresses, furniture, oil cloth which was also called tarry toot. It burned great, it was someone's floor matting. We used to put it in the National Health tins with a wire on and make a fire inside – then we swung them around. We also used the tins to catch fish in Leazes Park – there must be thousands of tins where kids have chucked them in. We made fishing nets with old bits of muslin on a stick."

Kenneth Scott on a swing in Nunsmoor Park.

"My dad died in 1970 and mam moved back to Westmorland Road, she was the first in and last out – built in 1980 and knocked down by 1999, there was nothing wrong with them. The outsides had all been refurbished and the insides were still brand new. There were 6ft sliding doors and we could sit on the balcony. I remember watching the Battle of Britain memorial flight going to the Sunderland Air Show and the Red Arrows. They pulled them down and haven't built anything in their place. Over a thousand houses from the Old Hall Social Club on Edward Gardens right along to St Michael's Church, all gone. Our Kenneth lived on Buddle Road when he got married. New houses were being built so he moved in to number 33 Buddle Road. Esther Rantzen came to the area and my brother and others campaigned to have a children's park built, but it's all gone now. There are factory units standing empty too."

The first job that Frank took on was as an apprentice joiner for John Porter of St Lawrence Road. He travelled around Newcastle looking for a start as an apprentice. Within a week he secured a position with the police force. "I served with the special constabulary for twenty two years from 1979-2003. My first base was at Newburn/Westerhope and then the city centre. I retired at rank of area commandant at Clifford Street in Byker."

He was married to Edna Marie (née Burrell) in 1972 at St Bede's Church. The couple have two daughters, Victoria and Alix. Alix swam for the city of Newcastle and she also became a national swimmer for England and Great Britain in 1997 was in the European Games.

Frank Scott riding his pedal bike on Elswick Row.

From Elswick Park to Vickers
by Gladys Fletcher (née Charlton)

Gladys Charlton was born in 1934 in Panmure Street, Elswick. Her parents were Eleanor and Robert. She was the youngest of four, Alice, Tommy and Myra. "We loved to play in Elswick Park in the pool. There was an aviary with all sorts of birds to look at. But I never got to see what the big house that stood in the grounds was like inside. We used to play in the low park – there wasn't much in there. We could climb up from the bottom to the top, we called it "The Little Hills" but it wasn't very high. We went on the witch's hat and the tea pot lid roundabout. During the war there were barrage balloons in the park."

Gladys attended Westmorland and Elswick Schools. "I talked too much at Westmorland, it was a good school and I played netball at Elswick Road School. I was the shooter – it was my job to score the goals. I always went to St Stephen's Church hall. I could swing on the bars and jump over the horse. I was in the girls' brigade. There were marches once a month for the church service, I wore a navy uniform."

She remembers that her mother baked for the family and her dad worked on repairs in the home. "Family life wasn't the same as it is now. When we were young, the adults sat down to eat first – washed the dishes – then it was the young children's turn to eat when we had company. Dad cobbled shoes on a last and mam baked bread, cooked mince and tattie pie or ham and egg. She made the most lovely Victoria sponge and Christmas cakes. She baked a separate one for me sometimes. Mam could sew, knit and make clippy mats. But, as long as my family is comfortable, that's enough for me."

An old witch's hat style roundabout. Children had to be careful that their fingers weren't in the way as the circle seat crashed against the centre pole.

Gladys remembered some of the shops in the area. "There was a shop in Scotswood at the bottom of Lister Street and Fowberry Crescent. Marky Davidson sold bone china tea sets, sandshoes, nails, scones, bacon. He sold children's boots. He had things hanging from the ceiling. Blaydon Stores were on Fowberry and a butcher's shop at the beginning of the crescent. Round the corner on Denton Road, there was a drapery shop it belonged to Blaydon Stores."

Jobs that Gladys has worked at include Scott and Turner (which became Andrews Liver Salts) and Bird's Laundry. "I also worked at Vickers 39 Shop – I was a driller. I drilled little holes in a firing pin for a gun. It was mostly women in the factory. The only men who worked there were fitters – if the machine broke down they'd come and fix them. It wasn't heavy machinery – capstans, drillers, borers, we all stuck to our own machine. We all made good friendships. After work we mainly went to the cinemas – the Regal, the Pavilion and the Stoll at the bottom of Westgate Road. We danced

Gladys as a child when she was evacuated to Flimby in 1939. She is sitting on the wall in a beautiful garden with her teddy and pram.

The Scotswood Branch of the Blaydon District Co-op. The memorial of the Great War now stands in the grounds of St Margaret's Church in Scotswood.

at the Brighton, Milvain and Oxford. But after I got married we went to the Rex and Rialto. I loved the Doris Day and George Raft films. We always had to stand in a queue. When we came out we had to stand for the Queen."

Gladys met her husband to be Gordon Fletcher. "He was born in 1932 and lived at 9 Blackett Terrace. There were two rows of terraced houses at the back of the Scotswood Club. The first Row was Ridley Terrace. When he left school he worked as a milkman. After he came out of the army he became a labourer on the buildings at Blaydon Power Station. We were married in 1955 and lived on Denton Road. Our son Gordon was born in 1956, he went to Denton Road, Lower Whickham then to John Marlay Upper Schools. Peter was born in 1960 and he went to Broadwood and then on to John Marlay Upper School."

Gladys worked at schools for twenty five years. "When I first started at 1965 I was at Rutherford Boys Grammar School on the West Road, then I went to Broadwood. I just worked fifteen hours setting the tables, serving the dinners then washing the dishes and putting them away. It was heavy work, because you just had a short time to do all of the work. At Broadwood there were two sittings so it all had to be cleared away and set up again for the juniors coming in. When my two lads were old enough they asked if I would go in full time. We all worked well together and at Christmas we went out for a meal. It was a good school."

Gladys lives in Adelaide House and enjoys going to her club twice a week where she meets her friends. "The caretaker and his wife, Darren and Tracey, organise dos together with Ann and Michael. We have charity dos, pie and pea suppers and table top sales quizzes."

Gladys and Gordon Fletcher at their son Peter's wedding to Ruth. They are standing in the grounds of St Margaret's Church, Scotswood.

Days To Remember

Left: A snowstorm at Adamsez in 1965.

Adamsez works were in operation from 1903 until 1972. The business was originally started by brothers Moses and Samuel Adams who made sewage treatment equipment and sanitary ware in York and Leeds. In 1858 the Benwell Water Works were commissioned to supply a 6 million gallon reservoir and pumping station for Newcastle & Gateshead Water Company.

Left: Outside Mrs Sparrow's shop on Helen Street. Look at how smartly turned out the children are. This is from Joan Berry's collection of photos.

Michael Senior and pal sitting in Hodgkin Park. Notice the fashionable style of the pram.

Stella Murray School of dancing on Bentinck Road around 1930. Maud Walton (Des Walton's sister in law) played the piano.

Todd's Nook School, Form 3a in 1951. The teacher is Mrs Smith. Back row, from left to right: Jimmy Birkett, John Patterson, Dougie Findley, Neville Thompson, Alan Taylor, Billy Johnson, Eddy Humble, Derrick Huntington, George McKenna, Terry Turner, Norman Holland. Middle row: Raymond Porter, Victor Wilson, Evelyn Hogg. Marcia Morton, Valerie Chalmers, Sylvia Pearson, Doris Brown, Mavis Nairn, Maureen Foster, Tom ?, George Graham. Front row: Irene Purvis, Irene Ferguson, Irene Buckingham, Brenda Turnbull, Ann Glynn, Mrs Smith, Doreen Budd, Pauline McEwan, Joyce Hunter.

Above: Kath Senior (née Wright) on her wedding day in 1965. She was a tailoress and had her own business providing beautiful gowns for brides throughout Newcastle. From left to right: Iris Woodhouse, Maureen Armstrong, Kath in her hand made white satin dress, Elizabeth Dosh and Hazel ?

Right: Can you remember winters like these? Folks had to dig themselves out of their homes. Look at the snow on the bottom of this lady's coat!

The last Christmas before everyone moved out of the area at the end of 1965. Johnny Cannell wearing football strip, sister Janice to the right holding a tray. Mark Benson in cowboy suit. Isabelle Ralph (née Wandless) in dark cardigan back left. Doreen Grieve wearing white straw hat and a dressing gown as "Midnight in China" at the back. Mary Grieve and Kitty Yeoman also pictured. Photo taken end of Buddle Road standing on Atkinson Road. Councillor Connie Lewcock judged the fancy dress competition.

Jimmy Grieve standing at the back door of 70 Edward Gardens wearing his cowboy hat in the 1960s.

George Grieve in the back lane of Edward Gardens. His sister Doreen nearby holding her doll with Buddle Road back lane behind.

The 1962 Blaydon Races celebrations. May Wandless is wearing a half apron. Joyce Cairns is seated next to her wearing white holding her baby grandson Geoffrey. At the front in a dark top and blonde hair is Margaret Burnett. Mary and George Best are also pictured.

Right: Harry Clift and his mate stepping out along Scotswood Road on a night out. Notice how vibrant the area looks in contrast to the deserted atmosphere of today.

Community Folks

Here are a selection of photographs that show what a thriving community we have in the West End today.

Red Watch at Colby Court Fire Station. The service actively encourages community involvement from schools, nurseries and groups throughout the area. From left to right: Tony O'Donnell, Ian Henderson, Brian Waugh, Andy Lane, Kate Fullen, Mick Mangan, Mick Thompson, Chris Docherty and Ian Warbrick.

Tracy and Steve Bonner run their business together – Adelaide Butchers. Their Benwell Belta is the best money can buy, check it out!

Ronnie Wilkinson guides the children to St Bede's School across Whickham View. He is a well known character in the community. He is also a popular figure at the Springbank Social Club.

ne1 fm staff and volunteers. ne1 fm – on radio frequency 102.5 – is a full time community radio station which features music, local writers, sports, open mic slots and much more. With varying times ranging from 8 am - 9 pm. Training to use equipment is on offer for volunteers. The above photograph shows the programme – The Elders Council, Everyone's Tomorrow – Today. The group broadcast on the first Friday of each month between 2 pm and 4 pm and the following Monday from 10 am to 12 pm. Topics covered are gardening advice, poems, stories, music and local information. Back row, from left to right: Phoenix Dark-Knight, Elaine Parker, Wendy Mizen, John Reid and Doug Leckey. Front row: Maureen Burrows, Jean Espie, Greta Heron and Steve Whitley.

This shop has been going for around 13 years and is known as Mick the Fish. From left to right: Simon Chipchase, Michael Johnson (owner) and Gary Hall. A poster was displayed in the shop showing that £510 had been raised for the Bobby Robson Cancer Fund at Bella Hull's funeral.

Community wardens Darren Boddy and Peter Thompson

Right: I took this photo at the launch of the Arc Project at St James Church. Locals were asked to create pairs of knitted or felt work animals. From left to right Elsie Marshall, Reverend Catherine Pickford, team rector, Gail Wilson and Reverend Peter Wilson and Susan Green.

Alma Wheeler at the West End Library. She was named after the Alma Inn which her parents ran. Alma is a prominent member of the community who is involved in lots of teaching projects. Alma was one of the contributors in the book 'Women's Lives' sharing her memories of being brought up in Scotswood. The book was part of a project by Riverside Women's Group.

The Park Centre provide support for locals – it is a hub for meetings and is used by Newcastle Futures, Social Services, lunch clubs, cookery sessions in the community kitchen, advice on nutrition, over 50s groups, weaning advice for young mothers and much more. Rona Simpson is pictured with one of the vegetable packs which are for sale at the centre.

Right: Andy Rodgers, Reggie Wood and Eric Horden in Andy's cabin. Notice the pigeon baskets behind the pals. As well as keeping birds, Reggie goes to races and also has an allotment where he grows vegetables. Andy jokes about Reggie's enthusiasm for his pigeons "You might miss him if you call at the aviary – he's only here from eight in the morning until eight at night!"

Acknowledgements

I didn't think that I would have the energy to attempt another memories book, but here I go again. As usual Des Walton was always available to give advice, provide information and for his suggestion for the title for this book. Andrew Clark was there for support and advice.

Members at West Newcastle Picture History Collection: Mike Young, Fred Millican, Harry Bennett, Linda Sutton, Bill Stewart, Sharon Clarke, Edward Bieganowski.

Volunteers from Westgate Past: Dennis Carss, Bill Rosser, Arthur Frelford, Terry Sutton, John Lowry, Edward Wiffin, Peter Hemy, Laura Thursby.

West End Library, Fenham Library and staff for allowing me to use interview rooms, offering support and information. To Mike Young and Derek Allen, photographers who supplied their own images.

Judith Green, Alison Flanaghan Wood, Richard Bliss and Ellen Phethean for including me in community projects.

Riverside Community Health Project and St James' Church staff and volunteers for including me in launches, projects and local events.

I'd like to thank all of the folks in Benwell, Scotswood, Arthur's Hill and Elswick who have posed for photos and shared their precious family photos with me.

Armstrong Whitworth at Scotswood was one of the most extensive steam and diesel, marine and general engineering works in the country. From 1919 they were a locomotive building establishment. Armaments were the chief products during the Second World War.